FORFEIT

FORFEIT

MITCHELL
SYMONS

Virgin

First published in Great Britain in 1986 by Virgin Books, 328 Kensal Road, London W10 5XJ

ISBN 0 86369 181 1

Made and Printed in Great Britain by Richard Clay Ltd, Bungay, Suffolk

Typeset by Keyline Graphics, London NW6

Cover, design and illustrations by Sue Walliker

Distributed by Arrow Books

Contents

FORFEIT

INTRODUCTION

Quizzes are all very well but they never actually seem to lead anywhere. Okay, so you can establish – up to a point – that your knowledge of sport is better than someone else's knowledge of cinema: you might even win a few pounds on the strength of it. For the most part, though, it's just like being back at school – except that you don't get into trouble for getting the answer wrong. Until now . . .

Forfeit contains 1,000 questions in ten sections, each of which is divided into ten sets. Each set has a forfeit. Within each section, the sets and the forfeits become progressively harder.

The first rule of *Forfeit* is that there are no rules. As such. However, I do have one or two suggestions:

1 Choose a section and select a set from that section (set 1 is the easiest, set 10 the hardest).
2 Agree with your opponent(s) that you will – sight unseen – bind yourselves to comply with the prescribed forfeit. This agreement can be forged in blood if it is absolutely necessary.
3 Use pens and paper – it can prevent arguments when checking the answers.
4 As a variation, with the harder sets, fix a score (eg 7 out of 10) above which no one has to do the forfeit or below which everyone has to do the forfeit.
5 Whether an answer is correct or not is up to the person asking the question and/or anyone else present but do allow some leeway. If the answer is 'a game of marbles' and someone answers 'the game of marbles', you should let them have it. Unless you hate them a lot.
6 Agree before you start that, whatever happens during the game, you will remain friends . . .

It only remains for me to thank Nick and Fiona for inspiring the book, Dad for his help with information, Shyama for her help with forfeits, Ray and Steve for explaining the difference between 'what' and 'which', Jane for explaining how they got it wrong, Cat for all her help, advice and commitment and Penny for her unlimited support, tea and sympathy and for allowing me to try out most of the forfeits on her . . .

FORFEIT

MOVIES

FORFEIT
MOVIES

Set 1

1 What is the name of the nightclub in *La Cage Aux Folles*?

2 In which of the *Mad Max* series was Max 'Beyond Thunderdome'?

3 Which member of 'The Magnificent Seven' was also a 'Man from U.N.C.L.E.'?

4 How many von Trapp children did Maria become governess to in *The Sound of Music*?

5 Who got killed in *Butch Cassidy and the Sundance Kid* but made it through the *Three Days of the Condor*?

6 Which movie – featuring him as a Cockney lothario – helped make Michael Caine famous?

7 Who played the title role in the 1977 movie *Julia*?

8 How many Mads in *It's A Mad, Mad . . . World*?

9 Who escaped in *The Great Escape* only to see his wife and daughter raped in *Death Wish*?

10 What did Sir Laurence Olivier, Sir John Gielgud and Sir Alec Guinness win that eluded Sir Ralph Richardson?

Set 2

1 What is Rambo's first name?

2 In Hitchcock's film *The Trouble With Harry*, what is the trouble with Harry?

3 Who 'lusted for glory' but not, when it was awarded, for the Oscar?

4 Which actor did Mia Farrow complain about kissing in *The Great Gatsby*?

5 Which notorious Kampuchean movement oppresses Dith Pran in *The Killing Fields*?

6 Which of the four Marx Brothers played piano in their movies?

7 Which infamous Senator does Tony Curtis 'portray' in Nicolas Roeg's *Insignificance*?

8 Which one of the following never played James Bond in a movie: Sean Connery, Roger Moore, George Lazenby, Ian Ogilvy or David Niven?

9 Which knight of the cinema has played Pinkie, Bartlett and Christie?

10 Which Peter Sellers movie saw him, Bernard Cribbins and David Lodge breaking out of and breaking back into prison?

Set 3

1 Which Frank Capra movie tells the story of a man who is saved from suicide by an angel who shows him what life would have been like if he'd never been born?

2 Which actor's appearance in a film set in Vienna was prefaced by the line 'Come out, come out, whoever you are'?

3 Which one of the three sisters is married to Michael Caine's character in Woody Allen's 1986 movie?

4 With which actor does Irene Papas (literally) sail off into the sunset at the end of *The Guns of Navarone*?

5 Who appeared with Peter Sellers in *The Ladykillers* and also in the *Pink Panther* movies?

6 Under what title was the movie *Here Comes Mr Jordan* effectively remade by Warren Beatty in 1978?

7 Which extraordinary person directed *Ordinary People*?

8 What was the title of the 1981 movie based on John Reed's book *Ten Days That Shook the World*?

9 After *Chariots of Fire* and *Gregory's Girl*, David Puttman and Bill Forsyth combined to make what film starring Burt Lancaster?

10 Who played Fletcher Christian in the 1984 remake of the Bounty mutiny?

Set 4

1 Which 'silly old moo' played a lady's maid in the 1958 movie *The Vikings*?

2 Which of the Beatles films was the only one to win an Oscar for best original song score?

3 What creatures does Indiana Jones confess to hating in *Raiders of the Lost Ark*?

4 At what age did life 'officially' end in the movie *Logan's Run*?

5 Which character did Harold Sakata play in *Goldfinger*?

6 Which Clint Eastwood movie was used as a police training film in the Philippines?

7 Which star of *The Young Ones* can be seen, briefly, in *An American Werewolf in London*?

8 Which famous American singer had a featured role in *Annie Hall*?

9 Who, as Margo Channing, warned everyone in *All About Eve* that 'it's going to be a bumpy night'?

10 Which Clint Eastwood movie saw him trapped in a girls' boarding-school?

Set 5

1 Which classic rock'n'roll song does Marty McFly play in *Back to the Future* that his audience has yet to hear for the first time?

2 Which actress starred opposite Sean Connery in the film *Robin and Marion*?

3 Who plays the family that Dennis Price extinguishes in *Kind Hearts and Coronets*?

4 Who won the Oscar for Best Actor in the year that Roy Scheider was nominated for *All That Jazz*?

5 If 'Mr Deeds Goes to Town' where does Mr Smith go?

6 Of the three versions of *A Star Is Born* – Gaynor &

March (1937), Garland & Mason (1954), and Streisand & Kristofferson (1976) – which was the only one not to win any Oscars?

7 Which Thirties star played Louis Pasteur, Emile Zola and 'A Fugitive From a Chain Gang'?

8 Who was 'At Sea' as a 'Doctor' but won critical acclaim as 'The Night Porter'?

9 Which actor went from a beautiful laundrette to a room with a view?

10 Which Lithuanian played a Yorkshireman in *Room at the Top*?

Set 6

1 Who found true love as 'Marty', the butcher?

2 Which classic movie about Hollywood contains the line 'Ready when you are, Mr De Mille'?

3 Which movie actor described his fidelity to his actress wife in the following terms: 'Why go out for a hamburger when I can get a steak at home?'?

4 Who, as Richard Rich, betrayed Paul Scofield's Sir Thomas More in *A Man for All Seasons*?

5 In Mel Brooks' *The Producers*, if it's 'Springtime for Hitler and Germany', what season is it for 'Poland and France'?

6 Which former circus acrobat took top billing in the movie *From Here to Eternity*?

7 Which Hollywood director featured his daughter Angelica in *Prizzi's Honour*?

8 Which former star of *Crossroads* played the police chief in the Comic Strip movie, *The Supergrass*?

9 Which portly, mumbling megastar was initially offered the part of Paul Newman's sidekick in *Butch Cassidy and the Sundance Kid*?

10 'Don't let's ask for the moon, we have the stars' was the final line of which Bette Davis classic?

FORFEIT

MOVIES

Set 7

1 Which of the three stars of *The Treasure of the Sierra Madre* – Humphrey Bogart, Walter Huston, and Tim Holt – won an Oscar for their performance?

2 Which Hollywood actress was never married to Bob or Ted but did once marry Cary Grant?

3 Which George Orwell character has been variously portrayed by Michael Redgrave, Peter Cushing and John Hurt?

4 Which star of *Un Homme Et Une Femme* was once married to Albert Finney?

5 Who is the only one of these famous men to win an Oscar for a specific movie: Winston Churchill, Graham Greene, George Bernard Shaw, Bertrand Russell?

6 Which TV presenter's father directed films like *Dunkirk* and *The Shiralee*?

7 Which American drama teacher made his movie debut in his seventies in *The Godfather Part Two*?

8 Who took the Greer Garson role in the 1969 musical version of *Goodbye Mr Chips*?

9 Who is the first of the featured actors in *Casablanca* to be killed?

10 What role did Sally Kellerman create in the movie M*A*S*H?

Set 8

1 Which Alex Cox movie told the story of a punk love-affair and a vicious stabbing?

2 Which Hollywood starlet of the Thirties and Forties was the subject of an Eighties movie starring Jessica Lange?

3 Which two films brought Marlon Brando Best Actor Oscars?

4 Who won the Best Actress award at the 1985 Cannes Film Festival for her rich portrayal of Rocky Dennis's mother in *Mask*?

5 Who actually won the Best Actor Oscar in the year that both Dustin Hoffman and Jon Voight were nominated for *Midnight Cowboy*?

6 What part did June Allyson play in the 1949 version of *Little Women* that Katharine Hepburn played in the 1932 original?

7 What rank did Lee Marvin hold in *The Dirty Dozen*?

8 At the première of which movie about the founding of the State of Israel did Art Buchwald declaim: 'Let my people go!'?

9 Which 'actor' attempts to slice off Jack Nicholson's nose in *Chinatown*?

10 For which movie (if any) did Sidney Poitier win a Best Actor Oscar?

Set 9

1 Which debonair Hollywood actor played the Mock Turtle in the 1933 version of *Alice in Wonderland*?

2 Which Oscar-winning Hollywood actress of the Forties and Fifties shared a first name with a well-known German car?

3 What was the French title of François Truffaut's masterpiece, *Day for Night*?

4 What bizarre, personal question does Detective Popeye Doyle ask potential hoodlums in *The French Connection*?

5 *The Turning Point* was nominated for eleven Oscars in 1977. How many did it actually win?

6 If you multiply the number of 'Days of the Condor' by the number of Sidney Lumet's 'Angry Men' and then subtract the number of Kurosawa's 'Samurai', what number do you get?

7 In the scene in the back of the car in *On the Waterfront*, where does Marlon Brando claim he 'got a one-way ticket to'?

8 Which actor looked after Lon Chaney Jnr in *Of Mice and Men* and Sylvester Stallone in *Rocky* but never managed to outwit Batman?

9 Which TV presenter, playing the part of a TV presenter, interviewed Taylor and Burton at London Airport in the 1963 movie, *The VIPs*?

10 What does Joe E. Brown say to Jack Lemmon in *Some Like It Hot* when Lemmon reveals that he's not really a woman?

Set 10

1 In which movie does Sigmund Freud psychoanalyse Sherlock Holmes?

2 Who, in 1933, produced the first movie to be made in full Technicolor?

3 What was the title of the first film Katharine Hepburn and Spencer Tracy made together as co-stars?

4 Which appropriately entitled, classic song did Elizabeth Welch sing at the end of Derek Jarman's *The Tempest*?

5 What was the name of the bank held up by Al Pacino and John Cazale in *Dog Day Afternoon*?

6 Which British character appeared in several POW movies – graduating to Senior British Officer in *The Great Escape*?

7 Which star of the 1985 movie, *Cocoon*, co-starred with Tyrone Power and Alice Faye in the 1938 musical, *Alexander's Ragtime Band*?

8 Which Woody Allen movie starts with a monochrome sweep of the New York skyline to the accompaniment of Gershwin's 'Rhapsody in Blue'?

9 Who played the role of Claudius in an aborted film which also starred Emlyn Williams as Caligula?

10 What are the first seven words Dustin Hoffman says to Jon Voight in Midnight Cowboy?

FORFEIT

TRUE/FALSE

FORFEIT
TRUE/FALSE

Set 1

1 The Welsh Grand National is run over the same distance as the Aintree Grand National.

2 On a standard typewriter keyboard, the letter K is immediately to the right of the letter J.

3 The first four numbers on the Access Card are 1234.

4 MCC, as in the owners of Lords Cricket Ground, stands for Middlesex Cricket Club.

5 Peter Shaffer wrote *Equus*.

6 Bernard Matthews, the 'bootiful' turkey man, is the younger brother of Sir Stanley Matthews.

7 Harold Wilson was once a don at Oxford University.

8 Mark Thatcher went to Oxford University.

9 Pink Champagne is a mixture of champagne and angostura bitters.

10 Brian Clough has canvassed for the Labour Party during election campaigns.

Set 2

1 Humphrey Bogart served in the United States Navy during World War I.

2 The South Pole is in Antarctica.

3 Shish kebab is usually served on a skewer.

4 West Berlin is the capital of West Germany.

5 The Beatles song 'When I'm 64' was once banned by the BBC.

6 Emily Bronte wrote *Wuthering Heights*.

7 A Chateau d'Yquem is a sweeter wine than a Chateau Latour.

8 Most new cars have front-wheel drive only.

9 Canberra is the capital of Australia.

10 Edwin Lutyens was a Dutch landscape artist.

FORFEIT
TRUE/FALSE

Set 3

1 Football clubs have to pay for extra policemen at matches.

2 In Fiji, Christmas is celebrated in June.

3 General Idi Amin was assassinated in 1982.

4 The adjective 'tonsorial' refers to the throat.

5 King Edward VIII was the father of King George VI.

6 Neil Sedaka's song 'Happy Birthday, Sweet Sixteen' was once banned by the BBC.

7 There is more daylight on 1 January than there is on 31 December.

8 The Army has won the Inter-Services Rugby Tournament the most times.

9 There are three times as many Friday the 13ths in 1987 than in 1986.

10 Eric Clapton once co-composed the music for a BBC drama series.

Set 4

1 There are more rounds played in the British Open than in any other golf championship.

2 The cricketer C.B. Fry was once offered the throne of Albania.

3 The next colour after green in the traffic lights sequence is amber.

4 Michael York's first paid acting job was as the Milky Bar Kid.

5 Cinnebar is a type of moth.

6 Prince Harry is Prince William's younger brother.

7 Bing Crosby once recorded a song with David Bowie.

8 Red Rum once won the St Leger.

9 The Dalkon Shield was invented as a contraceptive device.

10 Of the two boxing Finnegan brothers, Kevin was younger than Chris.

Set 5

1 Cambridge won the first five Varsity Rugby matches of the Eighties.

2 By road, the distance from Bristol to Cambridge is shorter than the distance from Leeds to Norwich.

3 Beaujolais is Nouvelle rather than Nouveau.

4 A championship billiards table is the same size as a championship snooker table.

5 Jeremy Thorpe once played first-class cricket.

6 All the EEC countries are members of NATO.

7 The Gunpowder Plot took place on 5 November 1661.

8 The world 'guerrilla' literally means 'little war'.

9 Foinavon was 200-1 when he won the Grand National in 1967.

10 Harry Nilsson sang the title song of the movie *Midnight Cowboy*.

Set 6

1 Tarzan's aristocratic title was Lord Greyfriars.

2 The position of winger in a soccer team statistically boasts the fewest sendings-off.

3 Five gallons is a greater volume than 21 litres.

4 The clock on *The Times* leader page is always set at twelve o'clock.

5 A pound of fruit is less fattening than a pound of chocolate.

6 Dave Lee Travis once played guitar on a Top Ten hit.

7 Pete Townshend's father was a member of the Harry Stoneham band that used to play on *Parkinson*.

8 1500 metres is a longer distance than 1500 yards.

9 The Twelve Days of Christmas end on New Year's Eve.

10 David Gower bats left-handed while Ian Botham bats right-handed.

Set 7

1 'Heartbreak Hotel' is the bestselling American single of all time.

2 Golfer Gordon Brand is the uncle of golfer Gordon Brand Jnr.

3 No woman has ever played in a Football League match.

4 Pasta is made from wheat.

5 It is possible to form the word 'quizzing' in a game of 'Scrabble'.

6 Judy Garland's real name was Frances Gumm.

7 Rod Steiger was once married to Claire Bloom.

8 The National Union of Teachers is affiliated to the TUC.

9 The suffix W on a number-plate means that the earliest a car could have been registered was 1980.

10 In poker, a flush beats a straight.

Set 8

1 The colour black was sometimes used to signify the live wire in a plug.

2 A champion flat-racing jockey generally rides more winners per season than his National Hunt counterpart does in his season.

3 The BBC TV globe revolves clockwise.

4 In real life, Wilfred Brambell was younger than Harry H. Corbett, his co-star in *Steptoe and Son*.

5 In bridge, Three No Trumps is worth more points below the line than Four Clubs.

6 The Beatles once recorded 'White Christmas'.

7 Marlon Brando's real name is Martin Brand.

8 Dr David Owen the politician is a cousin of Nick Owen the television presenter.

9 A gazebo is an African animal.

10 A train travelling at a constant 120 miles per hour will take 120 minutes to cover 240 miles.

Set 9

1 Paul Michael Glaser gets top billing in the titles of *Starsky and Hutch*.

2 Elmer Bernstein composed the music for *West Side Story*.

3 Sandown Champion was a greyhound.

4 In Australia, the wearing of safety-belts is compulsory for motor-cyclists.

5 Simon Callow played the part of the first entertainments manager in *Hi De Hi*.

6 Midge Ure was awarded the OBE at the same time as Bob Geldof was created a KBE.

7 On 4 January 1940, Neville Chamberlain was still Prime Minister.

8 Fred Astaire was once married to Judy Garland.

9 Imperial College is a part of London University.

10 Norman Tebbit used to be a commercial airline pilot.

Set 10

1 Sir Geoffrey Howe once worked as a news-reader for Anglia Television.

2 The top string of a guitar is usually tuned to the note E.

3 Leonard Bernstein composed the music for *The Magnificent Seven.*

4 Clint Eastwood once co-starred in a musical.

5 If an invoice including VAT comes to £74.75, £9.75 of the bill is VAT.

6 The Houses at Eton School are named after famous British Generals.

7 Prince Charles once appeared as a guest on Simon Dee's *Dee Time*.

8 Before becoming a rock star, Bruce Springsteen worked in McDonald's selling hamburgers.

9 The BBC TV soap opera, *EastEnders*, was originally developed for Border TV.

10 Sir Winston Churchill didn't go to university.

FORFEIT

CONTEMPORARY CULTURE

FoRFEiT

CONTEMPORARY CULTURE

Set 1

1 Which household bleach promises to kill 'all known germs. Dead'?

2 Which American singer wrote a biography of her singing father?

3 What do the letters 'CD' stand for when *not* applied to diplomats?

4 Whose novel, *London Match*, was the final part of his espionage trilogy and not to be 'larfed' at?

5 Whose *Past Imperfect* was updated in 1985 to include material about 'dynastic' ambitions?

6 Which weekly publication appropriately lent its name to a guide to 'Buying Used Cars'?

7 Which contemporary composer (and cellist's brother) went public in 1985?

8 About which margarine were 'questions asked in the Australian Parliament'?

9 What does 'barnet' mean in Cockney rhyming slang?

10 What did Bond do more than 60 times a day under Ian Fleming but not at all in John Gardner's novels?

Set 2

1 Which beer has songs written about it by a pair of now wealthy Cockneys?

2 What is *the* magazine of the advertising world?

3 Which British film star's life was re-examined in a biography entitled *The Other Side of the Moon*?

4 At the start of 1986, what was the highest mortgage on which a single person could claim full tax relief?

5 Which aristocratic novelist was remembered more than 39 years later in William Buchan's biography?

6 Which East Anglian businessman makes booty out of poultry?

7 Which star sign comes after Virgo but before Scorpio?

8 Which murdered member of the Royal Family was the subject of a 'warts and all' official biography?

9 Who played Rigsby and Reggie but tragically died after being in *Water*?

10 What activity takes Jane Fonda and others to the burn?

Set 3

1 What game sees winks squidged and squopped?

2 Who left the House for a publishing house and bought a penthouse?

3 Which Beryl Bainbridge novel is named after a flower?

4 Which chemist chain used to run a commercial lending library but is now more likely to sell cosmetics and cassettes?

5 What was the sequel to Jackie Collins' novel *Chances*?

6 Status Quo sang about 'Pictures of Matchstick Men' but what artist's paintings of matchstick men are worth a fortune?

7 How many of Enid Blyton's 'Famous Five' are genuine males?

8 What breakfast cereal is 'tasty, tasty, very very tasty'?

9 Which beatnik wasn't 'on the road' after 1960 but is still on hippies' bookshelves?

10 Who is the most senior clergyman in the Church of England after the Archbishop of Canterbury?

Set 4

1 What Nazi organisation is infiltrated by a Frederick Forsyth character who is anxious to trace his father's murderer?

2 Which blithe, bitter-sweet writer and actor was the subject of Sheridan Morley's *A Talent to Amuse*?

3 Which Australian novel about pioneering settlers became a bestseller and, inevitably, a mini-series?

4 In *The Beano*, what can Billy Whizz do faster than anyone else?

5 Apart from the hotel's directory, what book are you most likely to find in a hotel bedroom?

6 What newspaper is now incorporated into the *London Standard*?

7 What Japanese liquor is traditionally served warm in cups?

8 Which magazine reflects on selected BBC Television and Radio programmes?

9 Which cartoonist's collection was entitled *Very Posy*?

10 Which star model of the Sixties brought out a *Style and Beauty Book* in the Eighties?

Set 5

1 Which letter did James Clavell remove from a 'shotgun' to provide a title for a bestseller?

2 To which national newspaper's former editor are Denis Thatcher's *Private Eye* letters supposedly written?

3 What, according to the advertisements, is 'the growing-up spread you never grow out of'?

4 Which lone yachtswoman became a bestselling novelist?

5 Which TV chat-show host wrote a book in 1981 appropriately entitled *The Day Job*?

6 Just over how many standard cans of Coca-Cola would you need to fill a litre bottle?

7 Which stylish Style Editor of *Harper's and Queen* brought the Sloane Ranger to the nation's attention?

8 What sort of pedal-powered bicycle is used for stunts because of its tyres' deep tread?

9 Which alcoholic beverage is available in four different 'cups'?

10 Which Cadbury's chocolate bar was advertised by using situation comedy actors?

Set 6

1 Which board game for one has 33 holes in England but 37 holes in France?

2 Which Sixties pop group was the subject of an Eighties quiz book entitled *Ask Me Why*?

3 What chatty cross between a newspaper and a magazine was launched in 1985, price 18p?

4 Which TV critic mixed a parrot with Flaubert to critical acclaim?

5 Which American heiress and designer of jeans told her story in *Once Upon a Time*?

6 Which star of *Call My Bluff* wrote a book of girls' reminiscences of their boarding schools?

7 What subject does Malcolm Bradbury's 'man', Howard Kirk, teach at university?

8 Which opera-loving, great rock'n'roll swindler was the subject of Fred and Judy Vermorel's biography?

9 What is the nickname for index-linked retirement bonds?

10 Which celebrated photographer wrote the foreword to Koo Stark's collection of photographs?

Set 7

1 Which national daily newspaper was 'bought' by Conrad Black?

2 Who went from Page 3 to LWT to Number 3 but not to Dulwich?

3 Which radio show presented by Rod Hull regularly satirises the news headlines?

4 Which British playwright is a brother of a Sixties Prime Minister and a third cousin of the Princess of Wales?

5 Which puzzle was invented by Wilson Midgley and still makes people cross?

6 Who went to British Chloride from British Leyland?

7 Coming from Sloane Street, is the Royal Court Theatre on the north, south, east or west side of Sloane Square?

8 What went to Maine, London and Paris in sequels to a bestselling Richard Hooker novel?

9 Which stage musical was launched in 1985 and was affectionately known as 'The Glums'?

10 Where, precisely, in England is the Motor Show annually held?

Set 8

1 What is the name of Manchester's commercial radio station?

2 What 1985 Graham Greene novel was *not* – despite its title – a sequel to *The Third Man*?

3 With which building society did the Alliance form an alliance?

4 In which stage role did a professional wonder whether we felt 'lonesome tonight'?

5 Who became editor of the *Sunday Telegraph* in 1986?

6 Which recent Desmond Morris book took us on 'an expedition of self-discovery across the landscape of the human body'?

7 Which bestselling diet book was produced by a medical team from a major British university?

8 Which Spanish born artist co-founded the Cubism movement with Georges Braque?

9 Which monthly magazine (and holiday company) is specially designed for the over-60s?

10 What type of aircraft enabled H.W. Grosse to fly over 1300 kilometres in 1981?

Set 9

1 In which West End play did the erstwhile King Richard play a camp queen?

2 What is the name of Adrian Mole's friend Bert's new wife?

3 Which European country lends its name to a variety of whist in which each player receives 13 cards?

4 In any given minute, how many strokes will you hear on British Telecom's speaking clock?

5 Which ballet company performs every year at the Royal Festival Hall?

6 Which three screen stars did Roger Vadim write about in his book *Three Women*?

7 Which leading society magazine was edited by Harold Evans' wife and, later, by Anna Ford's husband?

8 Which Eighties pop group were described as 'Suburban Heroes' in the title of a book analysing their success?

9 How many different colours are there in a box of Bassett's Jelly Babies?

10 Whose 'True Stories' in *Private Eye* are illuminated by Bert Kitchen?

Set 10

1 The telephone numbers of *The Times* and Harrod's used to have the last four digits in common: what were they?

2 Of which opinion pollsters is Bob Worcester the managing director?

3 Which Sunday newspaper carried an 'exclusive' interview with the Prince and Princess of Wales, only to see it televised the same evening?

4 What is the brand-name sweetener in a can of Diet Coca-Cola?

5 By what more direct name is the card game 'I Doubt It' better known?

6 Which award-winning London restaurant saw the rise to fame in this country of the Roux Brothers?

7 Which former British ice-skating Olympic champion performed as an actor in a 1983 production of *A Midsummer Night's Dream*?

8 Who became editor of *The Literary Review* having had words with Lord Gnome?

9 What, appropriately, is the name of Waddington's board-game in which 'trust-busters' must break up cartels?

10 Which black American comedian's rise and (temporary) fall was described in *A Man and his Madness*?

FORFEIT

GEOGRAPHY, HISTORY & SCIENCE

Set 1

1 What oil is usually applied to cricket bats?

2 Starting with the smallest, place these trees in order of (average) height: redwood, bonsai, oak.

3 Who was the inventor of a miner's safety lamp who also discovered the element Potassium?

4 Who eventually got the hump (but not a horse) at Bosworth Field?

5 What is the predominant colour on the Canadian flag?

6 Which English county lends its name to a sauce popular with consumers of tomato juice?

7 Of which islands is Port Stanley the capital?

8 Who became England's Protector after the so-called 'English Revolution' of the seventeenth century?

9 Which two colours are mixed to produce the colour hazel?

10 What do the initials MD stand for when used after a GP's name?

Set 2

1 From which river in Cardiff do Welshmen derive their nickname?

2 In which season of the year do the Christmas Islands celebrate Christmas?

3 Which one of the following is not a chemical element: gold, silver, jade, platinum?

4 Which prison is less than a mile from BBC Television Centre?

5 Which acid, used by schoolboys to make stink-bombs, is represented by the chemical symbol H_2SO_4?

6 In what branch of science did Dr Desmond Morris first achieve prominence?

7 If the Irish celebrate St Patrick's Day, what do the Welsh celebrate?

8 From which United States Cape did Voyager 2 take off?

9 In which century did Sir Francis Drake see off the Spanish Armada?

10 In which London postal district does the Prime Minister officially reside?

Set 3

1 What is the Fahrenheit equivalent of 100° Celsius?

2 Which German city, the scene of the beer-hall *putsch*, holds a famous annual beer festival?

3 Which public school in Middlesex was attended by Winston Churchill?

4 How many twentieth-century Kings of England have been called George?

5 Which communist country had to endure a Cultural Revolution in the Sixties and a visit from Wham! in the Eighties?

6 In which county would you find the Cheddar Gorge?

7 Which famous TV botanist went to Tasmania only to spend his birthday in jail for his beliefs?

8 What is the test – satisfying bookmakers – to decide whether or not it is a White Christmas?

9 Which statesman was captured by the Boers at the turn of the century, escaped and lived to see the Beatles at Number One?

10 Which former astronaut fell to earth with a bump when he failed to become the Democratic Candidate for American President in 1984?

Set 4

1 Which foreign minister of Stalin's Russia survived the purges and outlived his boss – presumably because he excelled at cocktail parties?

2 Which Northern Spanish town was obliterated by the Luftwaffe but immortalised by Picasso?

3 Where in England would you find the hotel that inspired John Cleese to create *Fawlty Towers*?

4 What sort of oil is commonly mixed with petrol to power mopeds and lawnmowers?

5 What was seen in the sky over Hastings in 1066 and again 919 years later – but only with the aid of a telescope?

6 From which northern town did the most famous Hunger March start in 1936?

7 To which chain of stores was Barbara Hutton the heiress?

8 What is the principal chemical element in both diamonds and burnt toast?

9 To which part of the body does the adjective 'renal' refer?

10 What colour is the flower lily of the valley?

Set 5

1 Where in the human body is the metatarsal bone?

2 Which two countries are Prince Rainier's nearest neighbours?

3 To the nearest five, how many years separated the first and the second Great Reform Acts of the nineteenth century?

4 What insect induces sleeping sickness?

5 Which airport in Spain serves both Marbella and Nerja?

6 If Britain has a King or Queen, what does Oman have?

7 From which Berkshire village did the CND marchers annually set off in the late 1950s?

8 Whose face adorned the World War I 'Your Country Needs You' posters?

9 By what name were the waitresses at Lyons Corner Houses known?

10 Who was the last of the Tudor monarchs?

Set 6

1 Which island off the coast of Britain sometimes claims to be 'the thinking man's Jersey'?

2 What is the medical term for the variety of measles that expectant mothers must avoid?

3 Which one of these cities is the furthest West: Hereford, Liverpool, Stoke, Glasgow?

4 In which London square did the anti-Vietnam War demonstrators come to grief with the police in 1968?

5 In which ocean would you find the Seychelles?

6 Which RAF hero won his wings, lost his legs but still reached for the sky?

7 What metallic element – found in table salt – has the chemical symbol 'Na'?

8 What was the precise date of the start of World War II?

9 What illness – not necessarily the exclusive province of port-drinking colonels – is caused by an excess of uric acid in the blood?

10 Which King celebrated his silver jubilee in 1935?

Set 7

1 Where in Sudan was General Gordon killed?

2 If you returned to Britain with guilders and francs in your pocket, which two *neighbouring* European countries would you have been visiting?

3 Where in Wales did the Beatles meditate with the Maharishi?

4 Which country lies immediately due north of the Golan Heights?

5 How many years separated the start of the American and the French revolutions?

6 What is the metric equivalent of '20:20 vision'?

7 Which star sign is shared by both Paul Newman and Mary Quant?

8 On what river does the city of Lisbon stand?

9 By what name is Windscale known these days?

10 Which scientist made his name with bouncing bombs?

Set 8

1 How did Henry VIII's third wife die?

2 Which river flows past Shrewsbury Town Football Club?

3 Who was Foreign Secretary in the 1945 Labour Government?

4 What is the relationship between India's first Prime Minister and the current one?

5 If force equals mass multiplied by acceleration, what does mass equal?

6 Who was British Prime Minister when the Common Market referendum was held?

7 On what island would you toboggan down the hill to tea at Reid's Hotel?

8 How are the dates for both Easter and Passover calculated?

9 If you subtract the year of the battle of Bannockburn from the year of the start of World War I, what round number are you left with?

10 Who was the first Tudor monarch?

Set 9

1 By what name is the fish-hawk better known?

2 Which Nazi became a bestselling writer after being released from Spandau?

3 From what tree was the anti-malaria drug quinine developed?

4 Which chemical element was named after a relatively brilliant scientist?

5 Which happened first: the Charge of the Heavy Brigade or the Charge of the Light Brigade?

6 Which is the only South American country where the name of the capital city has the same number of letters as the name of the country?

7 Which peer pioneered science for schoolchildren?

8 Between which two countries do the Thousand Islands lie?

9 Going directly from Whitehall to the Strand, which London square must you pass through?

10 What is the main export of Nicaragua?

Set 10

1 Can you name any one of the members of the CABAL (a simple yes/no will *not* suffice!)?

2 In which American state can you find Mount Rushmore?

3 In which now defunct national daily newspaper did the TUC have a financial stake?

4 What is the formula for the Greek letter pi as used to discover the circumference or area of a circle?

5 Which country's corned beef was the subject of a major health scare in the Sixties?

6 Which of these Scottish cities is furthest north: Fort William, Oban, Perth, Aberdeen?

7 To which treaty did Queen Anne refuse to give the Royal Assent?

8 What long Australian river might be popular with gushing actors?

9 What is the capital of the state of Texas?

10 How many hours ahead of Greenwich Mean Time is Peking?

FORFEIT

SENSATIONAL SAYINGS

FORFEIT

SENSATIONAL SAYINGS

Set 1

WHO SAID?

1 'History is bunk.'

2 'You breed babies and you eat chips with everything.'

3 'All animals are equal but some animals are more equal than others.'

4 'A verbal contract isn't worth the paper it's written on.'

5 'God makes stars, I just produce them.'

6 'I want a movie that starts with an earthquake and works up to a climax.'

7 'The city is not a concrete jungle. It is a human zoo.'

8 'Ich bin ein Berliner.'

9 'In the future everyone will be famous for fifteen minutes.'

10 'Christianity will go. We're more popular than Jesus now.'

Set 2

WHO SAID?

1 In 1933: 'We have nothing to fear but fear itself.'

2 In 1981: 'They gave me star treatment because I was making a lot of money but I was just as good when I was poor.' (Clue: Good Money, No Cry.)

3 In 1973: 'I am not a crook.'

4 In the mid-Fifties: 'I am on the right wing of the middle of the road.' (Clue: he was a lord in those days.)

5 In 1968: 'Like the Roman I seem to see "the River Tiber foaming with much blood".'

6 On 22 November 1963: 'If someone wants to shoot me from a window with a rifle, nobody can stop it.'

7 In 1969: 'Comedy, like sodomy, is an unnatural act.' (Clue: pop-eyed comedian.)

8 In 1971: 'I would rather be British than just.' (Clue: Ulster.)

9 In 1980: 'Governments never learn; only people learn.' (Clue: an economist, but not a Keynesian.)

10 In the Seventies: 'There can't be a crisis next week. My schedule is already full.' (Clue: globe-trotting *diblomat*.)

Set 3

ABOUT WHOM WAS THE FOLLOWING SAID?

1 [He is] 'a cuckoo in the nest' – Margaret Thatcher.

2 'He is the nearest we are ever likely to get to a human Mickey Mouse' – Graham Greene. (Clue: a dancer.)

3 'He immatures with age' – Harold Wilson.

4 'In defeat he is unbeatable; in victory unbearable' – Winston Churchill.

5 'A good man fallen among politicians' – *Daily Mirror* leader article. (Clue: a Labour Party leader.)

6 'The crafty, cold-blooded, black-hearted Italian' – Winston Churchill.

7 'That desiccated calculating-machine' – Aneurin Bevan. (Clue: a Labour Party Leader.)

8 'She ran the gamut of the emotions from A to B' – Dorothy Parker. (Clue: Spencer Tracy might not have agreed.)

9 'He stings like a bee but lives like a WASP' – Eamonn Andrews.

10 'He rose without trace' – Kitty Muggeridge. (Clue: 'Super!')

Set 4

SUPPLY THE MISSING WORD(S)

1 'Power is the ultimate ****' – Henry Kissinger.

2 'I could eat alphabet soup and **** better lyrics' – Johnny Mercer.

3 'The only thing I really mind about going to prison is the thought of **** **** coming to visit me' – Richard Ingrams.

4 'Adulation is all right if you don't ****' – Adlai Stevenson.

5 'The worst moment for an **** is when he feels grateful and doesn't know who to thank' – Wendy Ward.

6 '**** is a fine place to live in – if you happen to be an orange' – Fred Allen.

7 'What, when drunk, one sees in other women, one sees in **** sober' – Kenneth Tynan.

8 'Barnsley Grammar School did for education what **** did for rabbits' – Michael Parkinson.

9 '**** – milk's leap towards immortality' – Clifton Fadiman.

10 '**** should be used on all conceivable occasions' – Spike Milligan.

Set 5

OF WHICH 20TH CENTURY BRITISH PRIME MINISTERS WAS THE FOLLOWING SAID? (NB: to help you, the order is chronological)

1 'The rogue elephant among British Prime Ministers.'

2 'As a man he was unattractive with unpleasant habits – always scratching himself.'

3 'In the depths of that dusty soul there is nothing but abject surrender.'

4 'He is a man suffering from petrified adolescence.'

5 'He is a modest little man with much to be modest about.'

6 'The best advertisement the fifty-shilling tailors ever had.'

7 [His] 'role as a poseur was itself a pose.'

8 'If [he] has a fault it is that he will smother everything with HP sauce.'

9 'We must kick [him] in the groin: we must be rough with him.'

10 [This Prime Minister] 'is doing for monetarism what the Boston Strangler did for door-to-door salesmen.'

Set 6

1 Which artist said: 'The genius of Einstein leads to Hiroshima'?

2 Which playwright said: 'The trouble is, Mr Goldwyn, you are only interested in art and I am only interested in money'?

3 Which saintly woman said: 'It is by forgiving that one is forgiven'?

4 Which gangster said: 'I don't even know what street Canada is on'?

5 Which chum of Sinatra said: 'You are not drunk if you can lie on the floor without holding on'?

6 Which British tycoon said: 'All my shows are great. Some of them are bad but they are all great'?

7 Which Marx brother said: 'Go – and never darken my towels again!'?

8 Which Royal said: 'I never see any home cooking – all I get is fancy stuff'?

9 Which Hollywood blonde said: 'Husbands are chiefly good lovers when they are betraying their wives'?

10 Which European blonde said: 'Men are beasts and even beasts don't behave as they do'?

Set 7
SUPPLY THE MISSING WORD(S)

1 'Strip the phoney tinsel off **** and you'll find the real tinsel underneath' – Oscar Levant.

2 'I have always said that **** is a short cut to the cemetery' – John Mortimer.

3 '**** are obsolete children' – Dr Seuss.

4 'I cannot see who is ahead – it is either **** or Cambridge' – John Snagge.

5 '**** is the city of perspiring dreams' – Frederic Raphael.

6 '**** are paid to have dirty minds' – John Trevelyan.

7 'To write a **** every day is like returning to one's own vomit' – Enoch Powell.

8 '**** is America's great contribution to marriage' – E. Fawcett & T. Thomas.

9 'I learn the way the monkey learns – watching its ****' – Prince Charles.

10 'The lady's not for ****' – Margaret Thatcher.

Set 8
WHO SAID?

1 'One reason I don't drink is that I want to know when I am having a good time.' (Clue: an Hon. but not really a rebel.)

2 'The essence of humour is surprise. That is why you laugh when you see a joke in *Punch*.' (Clue: not a *misleading* statement.)

3 'Success to me is having ten honeydew melons and eating only the top half of each one.' (Clue: A star is bored?)

4 'I always keep a supply of stimulant handy in case I see a snake – which I also keep handy.' (Clue: William Claude – initially.)

5 'An autobiography is an obituary in serial form with the last instalment missing.' (Clue: nude in Whitehall?)

6 'I smoke ten to fifteen cigars a day – at my age I have to hold on to something.' (Clue: a Sunshine Boy.)

7 'All comedians are anarchists.' (Clue: comic associate of the Beatles.)

8 'Fame is being asked to sign your autograph on the back of a cigarette packet.' (Clue: 'PS', his wife.)

9 'A cannibal is a guy who goes into a restaurant and orders the waiter.' (Clue: a mean fiddler.)

10 'A gentleman is someone who gets out of the bath to go to the toilet.' (Clue: a Yorkshireman – not Parky.)

Set 9

OF WHAT WAS IT SAID?

1 A profession: He 'is a guy who, if you aren't talking about him, isn't listening' – Marlon Brando.

2 A drug: It 'isn't habit-forming. I should know, I've been using it for years' – Tallulah Bankhead.

3 A royal scandal: 'God grant him peace and happiness but never understanding of what he has lost' – Stanley Baldwin.

4 'It gives you three extra hours to find your luggage' – Bob Hope.

5 'A man who has made all the mistakes that can be made in a very narrow field' – Niels Bohr.

6 'A man who doesn't know how to park a bike' – Spiro Agnew.

7 'Britain's strength, freedom and solvency apparently depend on the proceeds of a squalid raffle' – Harold Wilson.

8 A controversial film: 'Saddest movie I've ever seen – I cried all the way through. It's sad when you're 82' – Groucho Marx.

9 'The official journal of dentists' waiting-rooms' – *The Times*.

10 'A game for hooligans played by gentlemen.'

Set 10

WHO SAID?

1 'Music means everything to me when I'm alone and it's the best way of getting that bloody man Wilson out of my hair.'

2 'When you are courting a nice girl, an hour seems like a second. When you sit on a red-hot cinder, a second seems like an hour. That's relativity.'

3 'I just put my feet in the air and move them around.'

4 'You never really know a man until you have divorced him.'

5 'I can train any dog in five minutes; it's training the owner that takes longer.'

6 'Viv's friendship means the world to me.'

7 'If there is time left over, I fill in with a lot of runs up and down the keyboard.'

8 'The meek shall inherit the earth but not the mineral rights.'

9 'I always say, keep a diary and one day it will keep you.'

10 'I don't want to achieve immortality through my work. I want to achieve it through not dying.'

FORFEIT

TELEVISION

FORFEIT

TELEVISION

SET 1

1 Which one of the *Boys From the Blackstuff* invited people to 'Gissa job – I can do that'?

2 Who played the title role of Guy Burgess in *An Englishman Abroad*?

3 Who is mine (and Arthur's) host at the Winchester Club?

4 Which one of Little and Large once had a trial for Manchester City Football Club?

5 On which show does Jimmy Tarbuck offer odds for the contestants' answers and say 'off you pop, poppet' to the hostesses?

6 Who might say 'surprise, surprise – step inside love' to a blind date?

7 For what fictitious organization did Bodie, Doyle and Cowley work in *The Professionals*?

8 When Private Duane Doberman lost money to confidence tricksters in a poker game, which Sergeant won it back for him?

9 What was the first snooker series on television?

10 Which series of Roald Dahl stories was, perhaps unexpectedly, televised by Anglia TV?

Set 2

1 What car did Roger Moore drive as Simon Templar in *The Saint*?

2 Which former BBC TV newsreader might have found that presenting a chat show was 'Child's Play'?

3 Which TV company served the Midlands before Central?

4 Which soap opera was hijacked by Thames but safely rescued by the BBC?

5 Which former RAF pilot doubled money and offered opportunities to aspiring entertainers?

6 Who, as Richard, suavely bowled Audrey off her feet before doing a 'Nigel' as Neville?

7 Who, in 1985, went to Birmingham to help 'mastermind' *Pebble Mill at One*?

8 What was the full name of Lenny Godber's cell-mate in Slade Prison?

9 Which one of the original *Game for a Laugh* presenters stayed at the helm the longest?

10 What was Private Fraser's profession in *Dad's Army*?

Set 3

1 Who was the first Royal to be a subject on *This Is Your Life*?

2 According to *Spitting Image*, which actor is forever chasing a knighthood?

3 Which Monkee played Ena Sharples' grandson in *Coronation Street*?

4 Which children's TV programme starts off with the words 'Here is a house'?

5 What is the title of the Channel 4 series for senior citizens presented by Robert Dougall?

6 Which cartoonist co-presented *Ultra Quiz* with David Frost?

7 What daughter of a 'bishop' and wife of a 'saint' presents a rock show for Tyne Tees TV?

8 Who wasn't 'Good' when she played the title role in *Mistress* but certainly gave an excellent 'Solo' performance?

9 Who co-wrote *Marty* and then took a different 'point of view' to assemble the Monty Pythons?

10 Who was the only one of the original *What's My Line?* panellists to reappear on the show in the Eighties?

Set 4

1 Who revealed her legs to Eric and Ernie (and the delighted television-watching population)?

2 Which quiz show was the first-ever programme on Channel 4?

3 Who was the second Dr Who?

4 Who presented the *first* series of *The Sky at Night*?

5 Which TV company produced *Ready Steady Go!*?

6 Which *Spitting Image* puppet is constantly sticking something up his nose?

7 The editor of which weekly magazine presented *Scrabble* on television?

8 Which of the Monty Pythons 'left' the BBC for *Rutland Weekend Television*?

9 Who went from *Robin Hood* to Number 10 via *The Good Life*?

10 Who found marriage to Richard Briers in *The Marriage Lines* a lot more prudent than being married to a Torquay hotelier?

Set 5

1 Which Jack Rosenthal play featured the tragic life of pools winner Vivian Nicholson?

2 Which series starred Edward Fox as a monarch prepared to abdicate his throne for the woman he loved?

3 Who whispered the links in *The Old Grey Whistle Test* before a nightingale took over?

4 Which BBC presenter became a rally driver, ballroom dancer and snooker player in *In at the Deep End*?

5 What was the name of Budgie's girlfriend?

6 Which chat show host was once a schoolmaster in Giggleswick?

7 On what island does John Nettles play a policeman?

8 Who, in the interests of our entertainment, sticks his fingers up Kermit?

9 Who was the Starship Enterprise's only regular woman officer?

10 Who shone in Harvey Moon, rolled over Beethoven, but was much put upon in *The Young Ones*?

Set 6

1 Which long-running series of documentary programmes is frequently narrated by Chris Kelly?

2 Who went off *In Search of the Trojan Wars* but returned to compile a Domesday Book for 1986?

3 Who leapt from Sherwood Forest to the throne of Moldavia?

4 What is Jack Regan's rank in *The Sweeney*?

5 Which star name left the Peter Jay consortium *before* TV-am went on the air, because of her children?

6 Which actress helped to create *Upstairs Downstairs* and then starred in it?

7 What 'school' did Tucker attend?

8 What animals were slaughtered by truck drivers in *Not the Nine O'Clock News*?

9 Which father and son presented *Panorama*?

10 Which female presenter replaced Terry on his first holiday from *Wogan*?

Set 7

1 What BBC drama series was parodied by a situation comedy set in Nazi-occupied France?

2 For what programme did Barry Norman leave *Film '81*, only to return for *Film '83*?

3 Which actor was 'bent' in the theatre but 'out' on television?

4 What did Joseph Cooper play on *Face the Music* that baffled the deaf and non-deaf alike?

5 Who were *Three of a Kind*?

6 In which month of which year did Channel 4 first come on the air?

7 Which actress was a Miss at Grace Brothers and a Mrs in Albert Square?

8 Who wasn't a naked civil servant when he played the evil Caligula to Derek Jacobi's benign Claudius?

9 How many darts in total are thrown by the two contestants in *Bullseye* when they attempt to score 101 to win the star prize?

10 Who spoke the first words on both BBC TV and ITV and lived long enough to witness the birth of Channel 4?

Set 8

1 Who cried when 'face to face' with John Freeman but never when face to face with Eamonn Andrews?

2 What is the first name of Prime Minister Jim Hacker's Private Secretary?

3 Who left the house to feather his nest and ended up with his gal?

4 Name the investigative arm of *Nationwide* which shot off as a separate programme but was then called off.

5 Which former Fleet Street editor's daughter presents *4 What It's Worth*?

6 On what programme was Bernard Levin once punched by a member of the audience?

7 Which one of the Monty Pythons went on a *Great Train Journey*?

8 When Reggie Perrin eventually ended up at Amalgamated Aerosols, who was his *immediate* superior?

9 Who replaced Emma Peel as John Steed's partner in *The Avengers*?

10 In what critically acclaimed series did a character named Adam Morris lose his virginity, win an Oscar and find his vocation as a writer?

Set 9

1 Which actor's career was helped 'plenty' by his performance in *Jewel in the Crown*?

2 Who, along with the Two Ronnies, performed a weekly sketch for *The Frost Report*?

3 Who galloped to fame as a gourmet but then cantered off to church?

4 Which Australian gamekeeper turned poacher in a late-night pursuit of a zero rating?

5 Which actor was 'walking tall' in *Edge of Darkness*?

6 To which fellow 'guest' on *Parkinson* did Billy Connolly once reputedly say: 'If you bite me, I'll break your neck and his arm'?

7 What was the name of journalist Ken Wordsworth's column in *Hold the Back Page*?

8 Who were the two captains in the first series of *A Question of Sport*?

9 Which bestselling novelist created, wrote and produced the American TV sit com series *I Dream of Jeannie*?

10 Which lawyer wrote the television adaptation of Evelyn Waugh's *Brideshead Revisted*?

Set 10

1 Which actor's experience as 'Casanova' stood him in good stead for his part in *A Bouquet of Barbed Wire*?

2 Which soap opera about a football club featured a star player named Zac Bishop?

3 Which programme targeted at Asian viewers alternated with *Black on Black*?

4 Which one of the Hammond brothers found, to his annoyance, that his father had left his two younger brothers and his former mistress equal shares in Hammond's?

5 Who is the oldest inhabitant of the chambers where Rumpole works – although he prefers a desk to a cabin?

6 Which star of *It Ain't Half Hot Mum* found greater fame as the writer of *Me and My Girl* and *Don't Wait Up*?

7 Which pop singer was breaking ground as Viv in *Fighting Back*?

8 Which Fleetwood Mac song is played over the titles and credits of the BBC's Grand Prix motor-racing coverage?

9 Which detective series was co-written by a soccer manager and featured the then husband of a top comedienne?

10 How were Chrissie and Robin related at the very end of *Man About the House*?

FORFEIT

SPORT

FORFEIT

SPORT

Set 1

1. Who in 1985 became the first Briton since Tony Jacklin to win the British Open Golf Championship?
2. Which Yorkshire cricketer's Test career started in 1949 and ended in 1976?
3. Which cricketer turned 30 on his way from John O'Groats to Lands End?
4. What sport did South African Rugby Union star Rob Louw come to Britain to play?
5. Which English goalkeeper moved to a Scottish club in 1986?
6. Which English batsman is known variously as 'Rags' and 'Arkle'?
7. Which company manufactures the Barley Water consumed at Wimbledon?
8. What do Scotland play at Murrayfield that Ireland play at Lansdowne Road?
9. Under what name did Evonne Cawley win the 1971 Wimbledon Women's Singles Championship?
10. Which premier soccer tournament has twice been won by the Old Etonians club?

Set 2

1. Which is the only English first-class cricket county not in England?
2. Who, in 1985, burst through from midfield to become a leading West Ham striker?
3. Which number is directly opposite the 20 on a standard dartboard?
4. Which sport consists of riding, fencing, shooting, swimming and running?
5. By what sobriquet is cricket umpire Harold Bird known?

6 Which Swedish tennis player became the youngest winner of the French Men's Championship in 1982?

7 What 24-hour European motor race has been graced by the participation of actor Paul Newman?

8 Which team was beaten by the Chicago Bears in the first NFL American Football game ever to be held in London?

9 How were snooker stars Joe and Fred Davis related?

10 What is the unsubtle nickname of Australian veteran leg-spinner, Bob Holland?

Set 3

1 What happened to Graham Gooch in his debut Test Match innings?

2 Which country did Scotland have to beat in a play-off to qualify for the 1986 World Cup Finals?

3 Who beat Eusebio Pedroza at QPR to become a world boxing champion?

4 Which British athlete was Guinnless in the 1986 Commonwealth Games but still revealed himself to be a pure athletic genius?

5 Who was Britain's last men's world squash champion?

6 Which Welsh international took his time in leaving Anfield although he's always 'in a rush'?

7 Which London soccer club was 'unlucky' when defeated on penalties by Valencia in the 1980 European Cup-winners Cup Final?

8 Which horse 'danced' to victory in the 1970 Derby and became the top stakes winner for his year?

9 Which race takes place over 4¼ miles and can only be contested by students?

10 If, in a local soccer derby, the Owls were playing the Blades, in which city would the match take place?

Set 4

1 Which sport derives its name from the Japanese words for 'gentleman' and 'art'?

2 With the score at 9-3 in a frame of snooker, you (intentionally) pot the green ball. What colour must you now attempt to pot?

3 Which country boasted the rugby talents of Andy Mulligan and Tony O'Reilly?

4 Which former Chelsea footballer became manager of the club after becoming coach?

5 In what sport was the 1985 men's champion younger than the junior champion?

6 Which East European country regularly boasts the highest average number of goals in domestic first-class soccer games?

7 What was the unlikely result of the 1973 Rugby Union Five-Nations International Championship?

8 What was played for the last time in 1973 at Bramall Lane, Sheffield?

9 Which international cycling race is known as 'the greatest free show in sport'?

10 Who took the 1985 Milk Cup to East Anglia but not to Europe?

Set 5

1 Which American tennis player, according to Clive James, had 'the looks of Apollo and the name of a skin disease'?

2 In which European country was cricketer Ted Dexter born?

3 Which language degree did footballer Tony Galvin and cricketer Phil Neale both achieve?

4 Which 'gnome' led Essex to all the domestic honours in cricket during a six-year span?

5 Which country did Mike England represent at soccer?

6 Which Liverpudlian World Light-Heavyweight Champion boxer was featured on the album cover of Wings' *Band on the Run*?

7 Which country has won the Women's British Open Squash Championship the most times?

8 Which country topped the medals table of the 1986 Commonwealth Games?

9 Which Rugby Union club 'tigerishly' boasted the 1980 Grand Slam fullback and centres?

10 Which Indian cricketer has scored more Test runs than any of his compatriots – or, indeed, competitors?

Set 6

1 Bradford once had two clubs in the Football League: one was Bradford City, what was the full name of the other?

2 Which three Classic races did the filly Oh So Sharp win in 1985?

3 Which British world champion of 1976 and 1977 eventually retired with pins in his legs?

4 Who asked 'how do you spell kamikaze?' when commentating on Australia's batting during the 1985 Ashes series?

5 Which horsewoman won a bronze medal in the 1984 Olympics for the Three-Day Event?

6 Which recent England cricket captain once got a high score in the Civil Service examinations?

7 Which British male tennis player was a hit at Wimbledon and became a host in Portugal?

8 Which cricketing country hosts the Sheffield Shield?

9 How many of the first 13 Soccer World Cups have been won by the host nation?

10 Which East European country won 1984 Olympic gold medals for both men's and women's handball?

Set 7

1 How many wickets did Ian Botham take on his Test debut against Australia in 1977?

2 Which Football League club supplied both Alf Ramsey and Bobby Robson for the position of England manager?

3 What was the most common surname initial of the West Ham first team in 1964?

4 Who was the last Scottish-born cricket captain of England?

5 What happened to John Francome in his last race before retirement as a jockey?

6 When did Pele win his two World Cup winners' medals?

7 Which sport's Cup Final was televised (in London only) for the first time in 1948?

8 Which golfing Australian's brother holds the record for the most wicket-keeping victims in Test cricket?

9 What is the minimum number of darts needed to win a game of 501 in tournament play?

10 How many of the players in the 1985 Cricket County Championship played first-class cricket in the Fifties?

Set 8

1 Who couldn't captain the Cambridge University cricket team against Oxford University in 1982 because he was playing for England?

2 Which country did Argentina defeat in the semi-final of the 1986 World Cup?

3 Which England cricketer's wife wrote a book entitled *Another Bloody Tour*?

4 Which year saw the last of Red Rum's three Grand National successes?

5 In which year's FA Cup Final was a player sent off for the very first time?

6 Which Rhodesian-born tennis player was briefly Number One in the British men's rankings?

7 Which team was on the receiving end of Graham Gooch's first Test century?

8 Which one of the home countries provided the opposition for Kevin Keegan's first three international appearances?

9 Who was the first Canadian snooker player to win the World Championship?

10 Which leading darts player – known as 'The Ton Machine' – might have made a name for himself mending broken windows?

Set 9

1 How many Football League matches did Lawrie McMenemy play?

2 Which English golfer was the individual winner of the 1985 World Cup competition?

3 Which Test cricketer's brother played for Brighton in the 1983 FA Cup Final?

4 Who in 1986 only needed one delivery to prove his point but twelve to pass a record?

5 Which professional snooker player wore gloves to protect his hands when he worked as a miner?

6 Which of the current Football League Division One managers had the best goals-per-game ratio when he was a player?

7 Which racquet sport did soccer manager Ken Brown's daughter Amanda take up professionally with some success before becoming a coach?

8 Against which country did Gary Lineker score a hat-trick in the 1986 World Cup?

9 Which Spanish golfer twice won the now-defunct Bob Hope British Classic?

10 What is the only sport to be played at first-class level at Hampton Court Palace?

Set 10

1 Which two boys' public schools lend their names to well-known variations of the sport of fives?

2 Which one of the home countries was defeated 3-0 by Ireland in the very first ever men's hockey international?

3 What did Tony Simmons, Bernie Ford and Brendan Foster achieve in consecutive years for Gateshead Harriers?

4 What sort of weather wiped out a complete programme of London soccer matches in December 1952?

5 How many points were scored by Paris Rugby Football Club during a four-match tour of Britain in 1879?

6 Which American baseball star 'batted safely' for 56 games in 1941?

7 Which, now former, Scottish League club won the Scottish FA Cup for the first rather than the 'third' time in 1905?

8 Which British golfer was runner-up to Greg Norman in the 1986 British Open Golf Championship?

9 Which bowler took 33 Australian Test wickets in just three matches in 1985 and regularly gets batsmen in Notts?

10 What was the significance of the inclusion of Neil Bennett in the London Welsh team in 1976?

FORFEIT CONNECTIONS

WHAT LINKS THE FOLLOWING NAMES OR WORDS?

Set 1

1 Massiel, Dana, Sandie Shaw, Abba.

2 Tooting Bec, Hainault, Dollis Hill, Cockfosters.

3 Georgina, Timothy, Richard, Julian.

4 Run, Chevy, Paper, Steeple.

5 Savary, Lorean, Freitas, La Tour.

6 Redford, Moore, Robinson, Robson.

7 Mike, Rick, Vyvyan, Neil.

8 League, Ball, Special, Union.

9 Sir Matt, Sir Alf, Sir Stanley, Sir Stanley.

10 Shane, Madoc, Bowness, Holland.

Set 2

1 Shaw, Ross, Pillars, O'Toole.

2 Costain, Laing, Bovis, Wates.

3 Roald Dahl, Jim Slater, Ian Fleming, Prince Charles.

4 Harrison, Henry, Maddox, Dagenham.

5 Four, Spring, Flavours, Vivaldi.

6 Pam, Sue, Moira, Jan.

7 Fletcher, Prendeville, Munro, Worsnip.

8 Peter, Mike, Mickey, Davy.

9 Miranda, Orsino, Hotspur, Calpurnia.

10 Keach, Best, Blandford, Stonehouse.

Set 3

1 Chelsea FC, Capital Radio, Goldcrest, Mahatma.

2 Mick, Mick, Bill, Keith.

3 Galaxy, Mars, Milky Way, Marathon.

4 Member, Commander, Order, Dame.

5 Midshires, Yorkshire, Chelsea, Woolwich.

6 Lew, Leslie, Michael, Bernard.

7 Rees-Mogg, Evans, Douglas-Home, Wilson.

8 Hal, Philip, Charming, Town.

9 Moore, Sanders, Ogilvy, Charteris.

10 Hawkes, Freebody, Edgar, Spencer.

Set 4

1 Strand, Sullivan's, Guards, Dorchester.

2 Henry, Walker, Stewart, Young.

3 Mamie, Pat, Betty, Jackie.

4 Tim Rice, Clive James, Ira Gershwin, Bertolt Brecht.

5 Rushton, Cook, Fantoni, Booker.

6 Jim, Michael, Francis, Sir Ian.

7 Peter, Harry, Michael, Spike.

8 Carol, Hilda, Denis, Mark.

9 Persia, Tent-maker, Omar, Rubaiyat.

10 John, Adrian, Paul, John-Paul.

Set 5

1 Adam, Blake, Claudia, Dexter.

2 Jane, Catherine, Anne, Catherine.

3 Mustard, White, Green, Plum.

4 Raphael, Waugh, Worsthorne, Jenkins.

5 Bill, Sid, Tony, Griselda.

6 Richard, Mike, Conrad, Eddie.

7 *Bullitt*, *Breaking Away*, *Summer Holiday*, *Murphy's War*.

8 Wystan, Cecil, Christopher, Stephen.

9 Helen, Andrew, Harry, Sarah.

10 Michael Parkinson, Harold Wilson, Michael Aspel, Toyah.

Set 6

1 André Previn, Maureen O'Sullivan, Woody Allen, Frank Sinatra.

2 Huyton, Old Bexley & Sidcup, Finchley, Stockton-on-Tees.

3 World, Seekers, Model Army, Deal.

4 Benny Hill, Clive Dunn, Ken Dodd, Rolf Harris.

5 Chertsey, Marlow, Windsor, Twickenham.

6 Jenkins, Churchill, Prentice, Mosley.

7 Admiral, Cabbage, Skipper, Brimstone.

8 Green, Bryant, Jack, Wood.

9 Daffodil, Bluebell, Snowdrop, Primrose.

10 Master, Calls, Fly, Maid.

Set 7

1 Cradaul, Flownam, Einstenkranf, Gonk-Gink.

2 Attenborough, Weldon, Wenham, Cotton.

3 Sir Monty, Lord Derek, Ian, Sir Peter.

4 Paddy, Cyril, Alan, Clement.

5 Greece, Jersey, Poland, Norway.

6 Montgomery, Slim, Carver, Rommel.

7 Benny, Diana, Sandy, David.

8 Stonewall, Jesse, Michael, Pollock.

9 John, Mark, Simon, Matthew.

10 Beatrice Webb, Mick Jagger, Harold Laski, John Kennedy.

Set 8

1 Oxford, Bow, Coventry, Kent.

2 Mark, Emlyn, Nerys, Simon.

3 Bradman, Hobbs, Constantine, Sobers.

4 W, H, V, F.

5 San Jose, Belmopan, Managua, Tegucigalpa.

6 Puffball, Chanterelle, Magic, Blewit.

7 Jackie, Mario, James, Nikki.

8 Rowan, Chris, Mel, Pamela.

9 McEnroe, Kubrick, Bogdanovich, Streisand.

10 Heseltine, Cuckney, Brittan, Lygo.

Set 9

1 Mints, Lionel, River, The K.
2 Guy, Jonathan, Sally, David.
3 Leslie Bricusse, Heironymus Merkin, Joan Collins, Artful Dodger.
4 Sympathy, Nick, Beat, Red.
5 Edwards, John, Charles, Phillips.
6 Jemima, Sir Hugh, Harold, Lord Frank.
7 M.J.K., John, A.C., F.E..
8 Blue, Brown, Black, Pink.
9 Orange, Strawberry, Lemon, Lime.
10 Joe, Joe, Leon, Sonny.

Set 10

1 George, Conrad, Graham, Norman.
2 Cats, Dogs, Mouse, Lion.
3 Oxford, Wrexham, Crewe, Exeter.
4 Sir Peter, Sir Laurence, Kenneth, Richard.
5 Sarah, Norma, Mandy, Norman.
6 Red Rum, Rough and Tumble, Crisp, Greasepaint.
7 Walter, Jeremy, Bevan, Geoff.
8 Wigan, Brighton, Cambridge, Luton.
9 Ben, Alec, David, George.
10 Ken, Esther, Bernie, Janet.

FORFEIT

MUSIC

FORFEIT

MUSIC

Set 1

1 Which American singer was 'truly stuck on you' – 'all night long'?

2 How many trombones 'led the big parade'?

3 Who started the Eurythmics along with Annie Lennox?

4 Which American singer/songwriter was launched by Apple records and was, long ago and far away, married to Carly Simon?

5 Which smooth-operating chanteuse shares her name with a vicious Marquis?

6 The daughter of which pop star had a hit with 'The Kids in America'?

7 What boy's name did Prokofiev couple with an animal to create a children's classical masterpiece?

8 Which member of the Monkees apparently had to be taught how to *pretend* to play the drums?

9 Which brilliant jazz guitarist and one-time lover of Brigitte Bardot found himself asking incomprehensible questions to uncomprehending Miss World contestants?

10 Which Bud Flanagan and Chesney Allen song provided the title for a posthumous biographical show?

Set 2

1 Who joined the Beatles on keyboards for the recording of 'Get Back'?

2 Who composed 'An American in Paris'?

3 In which star's backing band did Nils replace Miami Steve?

4 Which song – once covered by Bryan Ferry – refers to 'the song that Crosby sings'?

5 What four words follow Jerry Lee Lewis's expletive: 'Goodness gracious!'?

6 Which one of the following words was a hit for the Commodores: 'Very', 'Still', 'Yet', 'Ever'?

7 Who was like a virgin and then married Sean Penn?

8 Which pop duo featured Jane Asher's brother singing a Paul McCartney composition?

9 Which soul singer tragically didn't hear on the grapevine what's going on?

10 Which Number One blockbuster for the Sweet had a rhythm and beat remarkably similar to David Bowie's 'Jean Genie'?

Set 3

1 What, in a vituperative song title, did John Lennon ask Paul McCartney that Horlicks has been asking for years?

2 Who played keyboards for the Spencer Davis Group, Blind Faith and Traffic?

3 Which 'policeman' sang the words 'I want my MTV' at the start of Dire Straits 'Money For Nothing'?

4 Which mouth-organist composed the music for the film *Genevieve*?

5 Which former associate of Jeff Beck found that 'Blondes Have More Fun'?

6 According to the Moody Blues, what does 'every good boy deserve'?

7 What musical piece is played by a bugler at army funerals?

8 Which pop duo were (not so) affectionately known as 'Doner and Kebab'?

9 What was the name given to Frank Sinatra's teenage girl fans?

10 What colour does Stevie Nicks usually wear on stage when she sings 'Rhiannon', a song about a Welsh witch?

Set 4

1 What did Tears For Fears exhort people to do in 1985 that Lulu was doing two decades earlier – and then again in 1986?

2 Which Lerner-Loewe musical contained the song 'If Ever I Should Leave You'?

3 On what musical instrument did Anton Karas perform the music he wrote for the film *The Third Man*?

4 With which pop group did Jimi Hendrix's manager formerly and latterly play bass guitar?

5 For which fictitious band do Guitar George (strictly rhythm) and Harry (part-time) play?

6 Which well-known singer wrote hits for the Monkees like 'A Little Bit Me, A Little Bit You' and 'I'm a Believer'?

7 Which member of the Rolling Stones acts as the band's diarist and librarian?

8 Which Scottish singer was 'discovered' by Esther Rantzen's *Big Time*?

9 Which Sinatra song starts with the words: 'When somebody loves you'?

10 If Brian Epstein 'launched' Billy J. Kramer, who launched Billy Fury?

Set 5

1 Where did the Flowerpot Men go that Tony Bennett left his heart?

2 Where were Simon and Garfunkel 'sitting' at the start of the song 'Homeward Bound'?

3 What is the name of Bob Seger's backing band?

4 With which band did Van Morrison sing before deciding to entertain 'us' on his own?

5 What did John and Yoko 'eat in the bag'?

6 In which year did bandleader Glenn Miller go missing?

7 Which comedian entered the charts by asking John if he had a new car?

8 Which band did Duran Duran's favourite yachtsman co-found in 1985?

9 In Edgar Harburg's classic song about the American Depression, what six words follow the line: 'Once I built a railroad, now it's done'?

10 Which rock band might have made Jerry Garcia's bank manager grateful?

Set 6

1 Which member of the Who composed 'Boris the Spider'?

2 Where, according to Edison's Lighthouse, is it that 'love grows'?

3 Which style-setter and, to some tastes, 'strange' dresser fronted the band Visage?

4 Which popular Irish rock band features a lead singer who shares a name with the first of Cher's husbands?

5 Which is the first planet on Gustav Holst's *The Planets*?

6 Which Scottish singer went from Eurovision to *Guys and Dolls*?

7 What, according to Steely Dan, was the outcome of Kathleen and Willie's marriage?

8 Which song was Elton John's first Top 10 hit?

9 Which 'supergroup' confessed to being 'scared shitless' at Woodstock?

10 Which one of the Seventies rock group West, Bruce and Laing was the drummer?

Set 7

1 Which impressionist made a spoof cricketing version of Paul Hardcastle's '19'?

2 Which DJ once crooned 'The Man From Laramie'?

3 Which cult band was Lou Reed in before he transformed into a solo performer?

4 Who was the composer of the Pointer Sisters' hit 'Fire'?

5 Who wrote the song 'Woodstock' even though she wasn't featured on the album of the concert?

6 According to Stealer's Wheel, if I'm 'stuck in the middle with you', who or what are 'to the left of us'?

7 Who was the youthful lead singer of the pop group Love Affair?

8 Who is Country & Western star Loretta Lynn's almost-as-famous younger sister?

9 Which New Zealand singing star once made an album with Nelson Riddle?

10 Who lived 'deep down in Louisiana close to New Orleans'?

Set 8

1 Which mass murderer once auditioned to be a member of the Monkees?

2 Whose album cover carried the ode: 'They locked up a man who wanted to rule the world/The fools, they locked up the wrong man'?

3 Which album did Emerson, Lake and Palmer name after a classical work of Mussorgsky?

4 What was the title of Frankie Goes to Hollywood's third Number One hit?

5 In which American musical did the song 'You'll Never Walk Alone' first appear?

6 If 'I'm the Urban Spaceman, baby,' what is 'the twist'?

7 For the rendering of whose music was the Bayreuth Festival inaugurated?

8 What Russian word provided the title for a Kate Bush hit?

9 What was the telephone number immortalised in a Glenn Miller song?

10 Which one of the following songs did Burt Bacharach *not* write: 'Alfie', 'I Say a Little Prayer', 'A House Is Not a Home', 'Little Green Apples'?

Set 9

1 Who, according to the Kinks, meets Julie outside Waterloo Underground Station?

2 With whose famous orchestra did Bing Crosby croon before going solo?

3 Which musical instrument was named after the Greek words for 'wood' and 'sound'?

4 According to the Mamas and the Papas, who's the only person 'getting fat'?

5 If you multiply the number of holes in Blackburn, Lancashire by the first digit on an early Manfred Mann hit and then add the number of the Route where you 'get your kicks', what does it come to?

6 What was the middle name of the oustanding composer who apparently aroused Salieri's jealousy?

7 Which poet wrote the words for the song 'Auld Lang Syne'?

8 Which pop duo included Alf who later switched back to Alison?

9 Which underground station was 'two and sixpence from Golders Green on the Northern Line'?

10 Where are there 'mirrors on the ceiling' and 'pink champagne on ice'?

Set 10

1 Where exactly in London is the street in *My Fair Lady* 'where you live'?

2 What did Frankie Goes to Hollywood achieve that Gerry and the Pacemakers achieved before them?

3 Which DJ had a featured role in the film *Ferry Across the Mersey*?

4 Which clarinettist's theme song was entitled 'Nightmare'?

5 Which American funk star has a father who once played soccer for Celtic?

6 If you divide the number of 'Hours From Tulsa' by the number of 'Little Boys' and then add the number of 'Days of the Week', what does it come to?

7 Which singer and actress married into 'The Court of the Crimson King' in 1986?

8 Who would 'rather be anywhere else than here today' – but anyway didn't want to go to Chelsea?

9 Who had a hit with 'It Must be Love' ten years before Madness did?

10 Who split up with Lindsey Buckingham and then asked Tom Petty to stop draggin' her heart around?

FORFEIT POLITICS

FORFEIT
POLITICS

Set 1

1 Which member of the SDP's 'Gang of Four' didn't make it back to the House of Commons at any time in 1983?

2 What is the Welsh name for the Welsh Nationalist Party?

3 Which leader of the Labour Party was once editor of the *London Evening Standard*?

4 What is Margaret Thatcher's middle name?

5 Which was greater: the Labour majority in 1945 or the Conservative majority in 1983?

6 Which deputy leader of a Metropolitan Council wore Italian suits – despite being a supporter of Militant?

7 Which Senator from Massachussetts announced that he won't be running for the Presidency in 1988?

8 What office did Sir George Younger hold before becoming Secretary of State for Defence?

9 Which party held the constituency of Orpington before 1961?

10 For which political party did Kenny Everett campaign in 1983?

Set 2

1 In the contest which saw Harold Wilson become leader of the Labour Party, which future Prime Minister did he beat?

2 Which former Cabinet minister started the Conservative 'Centre Forward Group'?

3 How many leaders of the Conservative Party have there been since World War II?

4 Which council leader claimed the police 'got a good hiding' at the Broadwater Farm Estate in Tottenham?

5 Which Trade Union has been led by Jack Jones and Ron Todd?

6 Jeremy Thorpe was to David Steel as who was to David Owen?

7 Which Canadian Party did Pierre Trudeau lead?

8 Which Yorkshire soccer team is supported by Harold Wilson?

9 What are journalists who regularly report proceedings at the House of Commons better known as?

10 For which party was Brian Walden elected to Parliament in 1964?

Set 3

1 Which New Zealand Prime Minister rather resented the sinking of the Greenpeace ship, *Rainbow Warrior*?

2 Which former Prime Minister became the 'Father of the House of Commons' in 1985?

3 To the nearest ten, how many Conservative MPs were returned to Parliament after the 1983 General Election?

4 How does the 'Chingford Skinhead' prefer to be known?

5 For which political party was athlete Christopher Chataway an MP?

6 Which Labour MP, first elected in 1964, writes columns for *Punch* and the *Guardian*?

7 Which Labour Minister of Transport of the Sixties couldn't drive?

8 In which political party is the Rev. Ian Paisley a leading light?

9 What was the title of Peter Jay's weekly political programme for Channel 4?

10 Who preceded Len Murray as General Secretary of the TUC?

Set 4

1 Who left the constituency of Derbyshire West for *Weekend World*?

2 Which right-wing Tory organisation might be the wrong way to start the week?

3 Which bank's collapse did Brian Sedgemore pursue assiduously?

4 Which late political broadcaster (and LSE professor) invented the 'Swingometer'?

5 In which year was Neil Kinnock first elected to Parliament?

6 Who became the youngest MP in the House of Commons when he won the Louth by-election in 1969?

7 Whom did David Steel defeat in the 1975 Liberal leadership contest?

8 What is the surname of the Conservative mother and son who were both elected to Parliament in 1983?

9 Which campaigning Labour MP won his battle for re-selection but nevertheless resigned?

10 Which Liberal MP for Yeovil used to be a commando?

Set 5

1 Which Office of State has been variously held by Roy Mason, Douglas Hurd and Merlyn Rees?

2 Which party did Monsieur Le Pen lead to ten per cent of the vote in the French elections to the European Parliament?

3 Who was the Environment Secretary when John Nott was Defence Secretary during the Falklands Crisis?

4 Which Labour Party leader once lost his seat to Manny Shinwell?

5 What was Andrew Faulds' profession before entering the House of Commons?

6 Which American political party usually gets Paul Newman's vote?

7 Which Labour MP, first elected in 1945, was affectionately nicknamed 'Mik'?

8 Which future leader of a political party was the 'Baby of the House' when he entered Parliament in 1965?

9 Which nineteenth-century Prime Minister shared a nickname with Michael Foot's dog?

10 Who was the Socialist candidate when Valéry Giscard d'Estaing was elected President of France in 1974?

Set 6

1 How many different political parties from Northern Ireland could technically be represented at Westminster after the 1983 General Election?

2 Which party won the 1981 Warrington by-election?

3 Which future Conservative Prime Minister was 'last in and first out of Suez'?

4 In the passage of a Bill through the House of Commons, which stage follows the Report stage?

5 Which MP – elected to represent West Belfast in 1983 – chose not to take up his seat in the House of Commons?

6 To which political party does the MP Dale Campbell-Savours belong?

7 Who became the first socialist Prime Minister of Spain after the death of Francisco Franco?

8 Which Senator ran for President in 1968 but was no friend of his namesake, the erstwhile Senator for Wisconsin?

9 Which comedian 'performed' a Party Political Broadcast on behalf of the SDP in 1985?

10 Which MP and former NCCL activist is married to Trade Union official Jack Dromey?

Set 7

1 Which British politician was ignored by Winnie Mandela and abused by President Botha?

2 Who was David Steel's predecessor's predecessor as Leader of the Liberal Party?

3 What Cabinet post was held by Denis Healey in the 1964-70 Labour Government?

4 Who preceded George Thomas as Speaker of the House of Commons?

5 Which Labour MP, the brother of a celebrated poet, moved the Bill to legalise homosexuality?

6 By what name was Lord Avon known when he was Prime Minister?

7 From which constituency was Dick Taverne effectively de-selected?

8 How many different Democrat Presidents of the USA were there between 1945 and 1985?

9 Who, in a 1986 by-election, succeeded John Golding as MP for Newcastle-under-Lyme?

10 Which MP might find that 'good things cost less' in Hove?

Set 8

1 In which year did Enoch Powell stand for election for the leadership of the Conservative Party?

2 For which constituency was Neil Kinnock first elected to Parliament?

3 Which one of Ken Livingstone's GLC colleagues was the first to enter the House of Commons?

4 Which Commonwealth country first introduced the practice of paying the leader of the Parliamentary Opposition?

5 What is the proper term for a short debate introduced by a backbencher at the end of the day's business?

6 Which Labour MP remained in the House of Commons despite his loss of hearing?

7 Who succeeded Neil Macfarlane as Minister of Sport in 1985?

8 How many Liberals were elected to Parliament in the 1970 General Election?

9 Which State did Robert Kennedy represent in the Senate?

10 Who stood for the Labour Party leadership election in 1976 but had died by the time of the next contest in 1983?

Set 9

1 Which former Labour Cabinet Minister wrote in his diaries of his relationship with Dame Evelyn Sharp?

2 Of the Churchills – (in chronological order) Randolph (1), Winston (1), Randolph (2), Winston (2) – who was the only one never to get elected to Parliament?

3 For which Party was Winifred Ewing elected to the House of Commons?

4 Which Conservative MP for Lewisham was also an Olympic cox?

5 What was the name of the surprise Liberal victor in the early Seventies Sutton & Cheam by-election?

6 How many MPs elected before 1945 were still in the House of Commons at the start of 1986?

7 Who preceded Andrew Bonar Law as British Prime Minister?

8 Who is the only Prime Minister since World War II to have previously held the three major offices of Chancellor, Home Secretary and Foreign Secretary?

9 Which woman Labour MP recently agreed to represent the interests of the fur industry in Parliament?

10 Who replaced Pierre Mauroy as France's Prime Minister in 1984?

Set 10

1. If you multiply the number of American Senators by the number of founder-member countries of the EEC and then divide that by the number of Prime Ministers since World War II whose surnames started with the letter 'C', what does it come to?
2. Who served as Secretary of State for both John Kennedy and Lyndon Johnson?
3. How, in 1985, did MP Ivan Lawrence make twentieth-century history in the House of Commons?
4. Which Chancellor of West Germany attended the trial of the men who conspired unsuccessfully to assassinate Hitler?
5. Which Conservative Cabinet Minister 'hosted' *The Price Is Right* on *Spitting Image*?
6. Which African leader's son was responsible for BBC TV's inaugural coverage of the House of Lords?
7. Who was the last President of America before Kennedy to be assassinated?
8. When MPs were first paid in 1911, what was their annual salary?
9. Starting with the youngest, place the following politicians in order of age: Willie Hamilton, Edward Heath, Enoch Powell, Sir Keith Joseph.
10. Which General Election of the last 20 years saw the zenith in the fortunes of the Scottish Nationalist Party?

FORFEIT

ANSWERS AND FORFEITS

FORFEIT
MOVIES
ANSWERS & FORFEITS

Set 1

1 *'La Cage Aux Folles'*
2 Mad Max 3
3 *Robert Vaughn*
4 *Seven*
5 *Robert Redford*
6 Alfie
7 *Vanessa Redgrave*
8 *Four*
9 *Charles Bronson*
10 *Oscars*

Selecting one of the assembled company as a partner, re-enact Bogart and Bergman's screen kiss in *Casablanca*.

Set 2

1 *John*
2 *He's dead*
3 *George C. Scott*
4 *Robert Redford*
5 *The Khmer Rouge*
6 *Chico*
7 *Senator Joseph McCarthy*
8 *Ian Ogilvy*
9 *Sir Richard Attenborough*
10 Two Way Stretch

Recite a poem (all right, a limerick) in the voice of an act*oor* – e.g. Sir John Gielgud.

Set 3

1 It's a Wonderful Life
2 *Orson Welles (in* The Third Man)
3 *Hannah*
4 *Anthony Quinn*
5 *Herbert Lom*
6 Heaven Can Wait
7 *Robert Redford*

8 Reds
9 Local Hero
10 *Mel Gibson*

Without breaking anything, do an impression of the man banging the Rank gong. (Removing your shirt is optional.)

Set 4

1 *Dandy Nichols*
2 Let It Be
3 *Snakes*
4 *30*
5 *Oddjob*
6 Dirty Harry
7 *Rik Mayall*
8 *Paul Simon*
9 *Bette Davis*
10 The Beguiled

Demonstrate to the assembled company how you cried when you first saw *Bambi*.

Set 5

1 *'Johnny B. Goode'*
2 *Audrey Hepburn*
3 *Alec Guinness*
4 *Dustin Hoffman* (Kramer vs Kramer)
5 *To Washington*
6 *The 1954 version*
7 *Paul Muni*
8 *Dirk Bogarde*
9 *Daniel Day Lewis*
10 *Laurence Harvey*

Do an impression of Clint Eastwood trying to get a telephone installed within one day.

Set 6

1 *Ernest Borgnine*
2 Sunset Boulevard
3 *Paul Newman*
4 *John Hurt*
5 *Autumn*
6 *Burt Lancaster*
7 *John Huston*
8 *Ronald Allen*
9 *Marlon Brando*
10 Now Voyager

Without harming anyone – including yourself – do an impersonation of Bruce Lee.

Set 7

1 *Walter Huston*
2 *Dyan Cannon*
3 *Winston Smith* (1984)
4 *Anouk Aimée*
5 *George Bernard Shaw (for* Pygmalion*)*
6 *Barry Norman's father, Leslie*
7 *Lee Strasberg*
8 *Petula Clark*
9 *Peter Lorre*
10 *Margaret 'Hot Lips' Houlihan*

Acting all the parts, do a one-minute scene from your favourite film.

Set 8

1 Sid and Nancy
2 *Frances Farmer* (Frances)
3 On the Waterfront *and* The Godfather
4 *Cher*
5 *John Wayne* (True Grit)
6 *Jo*
7 *Major*

8 Exodus
9 *Roman Polanski*
10 Lilies of the Field

Using other players as extras, do an impression of any song and dance from a Cliff Richard movie.

Set 9

1 *Cary Grant*
2 *Mercedes McCambridge*
3 La Nuit Americaine
4 *'Do you pick your feet?'*
5 *None*
6 *29* (Three Days of the Condor, Twelve Angry Men, Seven Samurai)
7 *'Palookaville'*
8 *Burgess Meredith*
9 *David Frost*
10 *'Nobody's Perfect'*

Demonstrate a baddie being shot in a Western movie. A black hat is optional but a realistic fall is obligatory.

Set 10

1 The Seven Percent Solution
2 *Walt Disney* (Flowers and Trees)
3 Woman of the Year
4 *'Stormy Weather'*
5 *Chase Manhattan*
6 *James Donald*
7 *Don Ameche*
8 Manhattan
9 *Charles Laughton*
10 *'Hey, that's a colossal shirt you're wearing!'*

Do an impression of Woody Allen having a fight with Sylvester Stallone. You must play Woody Allen.

FORFEIT
TRUE/FALSE ANSWERS & FORFEITS

Set 1

1 *False*
2 *True*
3 *False*
4 *False*
5 *True*
6 *False*
7 *True*
8 *False*
9 *False*
10 *True*

Cram a whole biscuit in your mouth and then, without choking, eat it and swallow it.

Set 2

1 *True*
2 *True*
3 *True*
4 *False (Bonn)*
5 *False*
6 *True*
7 *True*
8 *True*
9 *True*
10 *False (he was an architect)*

Sit through the next game with an item of underwear (preferably clean) on your head.

Set 3

1 *True*
2 *False*
3 *False*
4 *False (it refers to the hair)*
5 *False*
6 *False*
7 *True*

8 *True*
9 *True*
10 *True* (Edge of Darkness)

Act out the nursery rhyme of your choice.

Set 4

1 *False*
2 *True*
3 *True*
4 *False*
5 *True*
6 *True*
7 *True*
8 *False*
9 *True*
10 *True*

Give a convincing impression of a short-tempered clergyman explaining to a policeman why he jumped a red light.

Set 5

1 *True*
2 *True*
3 *False*
4 *True*
5 *False*
6 *False*
7 *False (5 November 1605)*
8 *True*
9 *True*
10 *False (it was an instrumental)*

Explain to everyone present why you didn't have sex last night.

Set 6

1 *False (Lord Greystoke)*
2 *False (goalkeeper)*
3 *True*
4 *False*
5 *True*
6 *False*
7 *True*
8 *True*
9 *False (6 January)*
10 *True*

Bare a part of your anatomy.

Set 7

1 *False*
2 *False (no relation)*
3 *True*
4 *True*
5 *True*
6 *True*
7 *True*
8 *True*
9 *True*
10 *True*

Balance a mug of cold water on your head for 30 seconds.

Set 8

1 *False*
2 *True*
3 *False*
4 *False*
5 *True*
6 *False*
7 *False*

8 *False*
9 *False (a gazebo is a garden building)*
10 *True*

Make the tea/coffee for anyone who wants some.

Set 9

1 *False (David Soul)*
2 *False (Leonard Bernstein)*
3 *True*
4 *False*
5 *False (Simon Cadell)*
6 *False*
7 *True*
8 *False*
9 *True*
10 *True*

Brush your teeth with shaving-cream.

Set 10

1 *False*
2 *True*
3 *False (Elmer Bernstein)*
4 *True* (Paint Your Wagon)
5 *True*
6 *False*
7 *False*
8 *False*
9 *False*
10 *True*

Someone in the room must make two requests of you. After you've heard the first one but before you hear the second one, you must reply yes to one and no to the other.

FORFEIT

CONTEMPORARY CULTURE ANSWERS & FORFEITS

Set 1

1 *Domestos*
2 *Nancy Sinatra*
3 *Compact Disc(s)*
4 *Len Deighton*
5 *Joan Collins*
6 Exchange & Mart
7 *Andrew Lloyd-Webber*
8 *Krona*
9 *Hair (Barnet Fair)*
10 *Smoke cigarettes*

You must challenge the strongest person present to an arm-wrestling contest.

Set 2

1 *Courage (Best)*
2 Campaign
3 *David Niven*
4 *£30,000*
5 *John Buchan*
6 *Bernard Matthews*
7 *Libra*
8 *Lord Louis Mountbatten*
9 *Leonard Rossiter*
10 *Aerobics*

Tell a joke in a foreign accent. If the joke is deemed to be unfunny or the accent unrealistic, you must take the rubbish outside.

Set 3

1 *Tiddlywinks*
2 *Jeffrey Archer*
3 Sweet William
4 *Boots*
5 Lucky
6 *L.S.Lowry*
7 *Three*

8 *Bran Flakes*
9 *Jack Kerouac*
10 *The Archbishop of York*

Do an imitation of a charter flight air stewardess.

Set 4

1 *The Odessa*
2 *Noel Coward*
3 The Thorn Birds
4 *Run*
5 *The Gideon* Bible
6 *The* Evening News
7 *Sake*
8 The Listener
9 *Posy Simmonds*
10 *Twiggy*

Peel an orange using only your teeth.

Set 5

1 *The letter 't'*
2 *The* Daily Telegraph *(William Deedes)*
3 *Marmite*
4 *Clare Francis*
5 *Terry Wogan*
6 *Just over three*
7 *Peter York*
8 *BMX*
9 *Pimms*
10 *Wispa*

Phone an old friend whom you haven't spoken to for ages.

Set 6

1 *Solitaire*
2 *The Beatles*
3 Chat
4 *Julian Barnes*
5 *Gloria Vanderbilt*
6 *Arthur Marshall*
7 *History*
8 *Malcolm McClaren*
9 *Granny Bonds*
10 *Norman Parkinson*

You must make five different 'wind' ('fart', if you prefer) sounds relating to five different foods.

Set 7

1 *The* Daily Telegraph
2 *Samantha Fox*
3 The News Huddlines
4 *William Douglas-Home*
5 *The crossword*
6 *Sir Michael Edwardes*
7 *The west side*
8 M*A*S*H
9 Les Misérables
10 *The National Exhibition Centre, Birmingham*

Invite someone in the room to tell an embarrassing story about you when you were younger.

Set 8

1 *Piccadilly*
2 The Tenth Man
3 *The Leicester Building Society*
4 *Elvis Presley*
5 *Peregrine Worsthorne*
6 Bodywatching
7 The Cambridge Diet

8 *Pablo Picasso*
9 Saga
10 *A glider*

Get someone to tickle your feet with a feather for 30 seconds.

Set 9

1 Torch-Song Trilogy *(Anthony Sher)*
2 *Queenie*
3 *Germany (German Whist)*
4 *18*
5 *The Festival Ballet Company*
6 *Brigitte Bardot, Catherine Deneuve and Jane Fonda*
7 Tatler
8 *Duran Duran*
9 *Five*
10 *Christopher Logue's*

Eat a disgusting sandwich (e.g. mustard or tomato ketchup) prepared for you by your friends.

Set 10

1 *1234*
2 *MORI*
3 The Mail on Sunday
4 *Nutra-Sweet*
5 *Cheat*
6 *Le Gavroche*
7 *John Curry*
8 *Auberon Waugh*
9 *'Anti-Monopoly'*
10 *Richard Pryor*

Do all the washing-up that needs doing.

FORFEIT

GEOGRAPHY, HISTORY & SCIENCE ANSWERS & FORFEITS

Set 1

1 *Linseed oil*
2 *Bonsai, oak, redwood*
3 *Sir Humphrey Davy*
4 *Richard III*
5 *Red*
6 *Worcestershire*
7 *The Falkland Islands*
8 *Oliver Cromwell*
9 *Green and brown*
10 *Doctor of Medicine*

Without laughing, do a passable imitation of a goldfish for 30 seconds. If you laugh, start again until you get it right.

Set 2

1 *The River Taff*
2 *Summer*
3 *Jade*
4 *Wormwood Scrubs*
5 *Sulphuric acid*
6 *Zoology*
7 *St David's Day*
8 *Cape Canaveral*
9 *The sixteenth century (1588)*
10 *SW1*

Imitate a known household germ for 30 seconds.

Set 3

1 *212°*
2 *Munich*
3 *Harrow*
4 *Two*
5 *China*
6 *Somerset*
7 *David Bellamy*

8 *Whether there is snow on the roof of the London Weather Centre*
9 *Sir Winston Churchill*
10 *John Glenn*

Invite the other player(s) to test your knee reflexes for you.

Set 4

1 *Vyacheslav Molotov*
2 *Guernica*
3 *Torquay*
4 *Two-stroke oil*
5 *Halley's Comet*
6 *Jarrow*
7 *Woolworth*
8 *Carbon*
9 *The kidneys*
10 *White (cream)*

Mime the metamorphosis of a caterpillar into a butterfly.

Set 5

1 *The foot*
2 *France and Italy*
3 *35 years (1832 and 1867)*
4 *The tsetse fly*
5 *Malaga*
6 *A Sultan*
7 *Aldermaston*
8 *Lord Kitchener's*
9 *Nippies*
10 *Elizabeth I*

Recite your 8 times table. If you make a mistake, recite your 9 times table (and so on until you get it right).

FORFEIT

GEOGRAPHY, HISTORY & SCIENCE
ANSWERS & FORFEITS

Set 6

1 *Guernsey*
2 *Rubella (German Measles)*
3 *Glasgow*
4 *Grosvenor Square*
5 *The Indian Ocean*
6 *Douglas Bader*
7 *Sodium*
8 *3 September 1939*
9 *Gout*
10 *King George V*

Lie on your back and touch the back of your head with your feet. If you fail, offer to make a hot drink for anyone who wants one.

Set 7

1 *Khartoum*
2 *Holland and Belgium*
3 *Bangor*
4 *Lebanon*
5 *13 (1776; 1789)*
6 *'6:6 vision'*
7 *Aquarius*
8 *The Tagus*
9 *Sellafield*
10 *Barnes Wallis*

Put a tea-bag in your mouth for ten seconds.

Set 8

1 *In childbirth (Jane Seymour)*
2 *The River Severn*
3 *Ernest Bevin*
4 *Grandfather (Nehru) and grandson (Gandhi)*
5 *Force divided by acceleration*
6 *Harold Wilson*
7 *Madeira*

8 *By the lunar cycle (lunar calendar)*
9 *600*
10 *Henry VII*

> Balance an uncooked egg on your tongue for ten seconds.

Set 9

1. *The osprey*
2. *Albert Speer*
3. *The willow tree*
4. *Einsteinium*
5. *The Charge of the Heavy Brigade (both were on the same day)*
6. *Peru (Lima)*
7. *Lord Nuffield*
8. *The USA and Canada*
9. *Trafalgar Square*
10. *Coffee*

> Invite one of the assembled company to lend you one of their socks which you must tie round your wrist for the duration of the next game.

Set 10

1. *Clifford, Ashley-Cooper, Buckingham, Arlington, Lauderdale*
2. *South Dakota*
3. Daily Herald
4. $^{22}/_{7}$ *or 3.14159*
5. *Argentina*
6. *Aberdeen*
7. *The Treaty of Utrecht*
8. *The River Darling*
9. *Austin*
10. *Eight hours*

> Put a spoonful of custard powder in your mouth.

FORFEIT

SENSATIONAL SAYINGS ANSWERS & FORFEITS

Set 1

1 *Henry Ford*
2 *Arnold Wesker*
3 *George Orwell*
4 *Sam Goldwyn*
5 *Sam Goldwyn*
6 *Sam Goldwyn*
7 *Desmond Morris*
8 *John Kennedy*
9 *Andy Warhol*
10 *John Lennon*

> Offer to fetch a (cold) drink for anyone present who wants one.

Set 2

1 *Franklin Roosevelt*
2 *Bob Marley*
3 *Richard Nixon*
4 *Tony Benn*
5 *Enoch Powell*
6 *John F. Kennedy*
7 *Marty Feldman*
8 *Rev. Ian Paisley*
9 *Milton Friedman*
10 *Henry Kissinger*

> Tell each person in the room something you really like about them.

Set 3

1 *The Bishop of Durham*
2 *Fred Astaire*
3 *Tony Benn*
4 *Field Marshal Montgomery*
5 *Michael Foot*
6 *Benito Mussolini*
7 *Hugh Gaitskell*

8 *Katharine Hepburn*
9 *Muhammad Ali*
10 *David Frost*

Do an impression of an elephant giving birth.

Set 4

1 *'Aphrodisiac'*
2 *'Shit'*
3 *'Lord Longford'*
4 *'Inhale'*
5 *'Atheist'*
6 *'California'*
7 *'Garbo'*
8 *'Myxomatosis'*
9 *'Cheese'*
10 *'Contraceptives'*

Play musical chairs on your own – without a chair.

Set 5

1 *David Lloyd George (Kenneth Morgan)*
2 *Stanley Baldwin (Diana Mosley)*
3 *Neville Chamberlain (Winston Churchill)*
4 *Winston Churchill (Aneurin Bevan)*
5 *Clement Attlee (Winston Churchill)*
6 *Anthony Eden (Bonar Thompson)*
7 *Harold Macmillan (Harold Wilson)*
8 *Harold Wilson (Mary Wilson)*
9 *Edward Heath (Harold Wilson)*
10 *Margaret Thatcher (Denis Healey)*

Tell the assembled company a (true) secret about yourself.

Set 6

1 *Pablo Picasso*
2 *George Bernard Shaw*
3 *Mother Teresa*
4 *Al Capone*
5 *Dean Martin*
6 *Lew Grade*
7 *Groucho Marx*
8 *Prince Philip*
9 *Marilyn Monroe*
10 *Brigitte Bardot*

Taking the first page of the book of your choice, read aloud backwards (the words not the letters). Continue with subsequent pages until you get it right.

Set 7

1 *'Hollywood'*
2 *'Exercise'*
3 *'Adults'*
4 *'Oxford'*
5 *'Cambridge'*
6 *'Censors'*
7 *'Diary'*
8 *'Divorce'*
9 *'Parents'*
10 *'Turning'*

Blindfolded, identify the other person/people in the room by feeling bottoms.

Set 8

1 *Nancy Mitford*
2 *A.P. Herbert*
3 *Barbra Streisand*
4 *W.C. Fields*
5 *Quentin Crisp*
6 *George Burns*
7 *Ken Dodd*

8 *Billy Connolly*
9 *Jack Benny*
10 *Fred Trueman*

If you're a woman, empty the contents of your handbag; if you're a man, empty all your pockets.

Set 9

1 *An actor*
2 *Cocaine*
3 *King Edward VIII's abdication*
4 *Concorde*
5 *An expert*
6 *An intellectual*
7 *Premium Bonds*
8 Last Tango in Paris
9 Punch
10 *Rugby*

Peel a lemon and eat at least half of it. Drinking half a Jif will do as an alternative.

Set 10

1 *Edward Heath*
2 *Albert Einstein*
3 *Fred Astaire*
4 *Zsa-Zsa Gabor*
5 *Barbara Woodhouse*
6 *Ian Botham*
7 *Liberace*
8 *Paul Getty*
9 *Mae West*
10 *Woody Allen*

If you're a smoker, you must not smoke for at least an hour. If you're a non-smoker, you must empty all the ashtrays.

FORFEIT

TELEVISION
ANSWERS & FORFEITS

Set 1

1 *Yosser Hughes*
2 *Alan Bates*
3 *Dave*
4 *Eddie Large*
5 Winner Takes All
6 *Cilla Black*
7 *CI5*
8 *Sergeant Ernie Bilko*
9 Pot Black
10 Tales of the Unexpected

Turn on the TV, tune it to Channel 4 and watch whatever's on for one minute.

Set 2

1 *A Volvo*
2 *Michael Aspel*
3 *ATV*
4 Dallas
5 *Hughie Green*
6 *Peter Bowles*
7 *Magnus Magnusson*
8 *Norman Stanley Fletcher*
9 *Jeremy Beadle*
10 *Undertaker*

Do an imitation of Sue Ellen ringing up to make a dental appointment.

Set 3

1 *Lord Louis Mountbatten*
2 *Donald Sinden*
3 *Davy Jones*
4 Play School
5 Years Ahead
6 *Willie Rushton*
7 *Paula Yates (*The Tube*)*

8 *Felicity Kendal*
9 *Barry Took*
10 *Barbara Kelly*

Do an imitation of Sir Robin Day shutting someone up just as they're making an interesting point on *Question Time*.

Set 4

1 *Angela Rippon*
2 Countdown
3 *Patrick Troughton*
4 *Patrick Moore*
5 *Rediffusion*
6 *Melvyn Bragg*
7 Punch *(Alan Coren)*
8 *Eric Idle*
9 *Paul Eddington*
10 *Prunella Scales*

Give a one-minute dissertation on 'The Operative Similarities' between Dirty Den and the Shakespeare character of your choice'.

Set 5

1 Spend, Spend, Spend
2 Edward and Mrs Simpson
3 *Bob Harris*
4 *Chris Serle*
5 *Hazel*
6 *Russell Harty*
7 *Jersey (*Bergerac*)*
8 *Jim Henson*
9 *Lieutenant Uhura*
10 *Nigel Planer*

Blindfolded, distinguish between butter and margarine. If you are wrong (or the ingredients are unavailable) give a one-minute discourse on ways to reduce the butter mountain.

Set 6

1 World in Action
2 *Michael Wood*
3 *Michael Praed*
4 *Detective Inspector*
5 *Esther Rantzen*
6 *Jean Marsh*
7 *Grange Hill*
8 *Hedgehogs*
9 *Richard and David Dimbleby*
10 *Selina Scott*

Make a one-minute speech extolling Selina Scott's virtues or, if you prefer, a ten-second speech extolling Terry Wogan's.

Set 7

1 Secret Army ('Allo, 'Allo)
2 Omnibus
3 *Tom Bell*
4 *A silent piano*
5 *Lenny Henry, David Copperfield and Tracey Ullman*
6 *November 1982*
7 *Wendy Richard*
8 *John Hurt*
9 *Six*
10 *Leslie Mitchell*

For one minute, wave your arms up and down in the air like a *The Price Is Right* contestant.

Set 8

1 *Gilbert Harding*
2 *Bernard*
3 *Richard O'Sullivan*
4 Watchdog
5 *Sir John Junor (daughter: Penny)*
6 That Was the Week That Was (TW3)
7 *Michael Palin*
8 *C.J.*
9 *Tara King*
10 The Glittering Prizes

Do an imitation of the TV newsreader of your choice unctuously introducing a story about the Royal Family.

Set 9

1 *Charles Dance*
2 *John Cleese*
3 *Graham Kerr*
4 *Clive James*
5 *Joe Don Baker*
6 *Emu (and Rod Hull)*
7 *'The Poet Laureate of Sport'*
8 *Gareth Edwards and Emlyn Hughes*
9 *Sidney Sheldon*
10 *John Mortimer*

Invite one of the players to bare her/his teeth à la Esther Rantzen and give you a love bite. If no one will oblige, you must go and clean the bath (for the next forfeit).

Set 10

1 *Frank Finlay*
2 United
3 Eastern Eye
4 *Edward (Ted)*
5 *Uncle Tom*
6 *George Leyton*
7 *Hazel O'Connor*
8 *'The Chain'*
9 Hazell *(Terry Venables; Nicholas Ball, then married to Pamela Stephenson)*
10 *Brother-in-law and sister-in-law (she married his brother)*

Position yourself above a quarter-full bath (warm water – we aren't sadists) and invite someone to ask you the next three questions in the book. If you get two or three wrong, you must lower yourself into the water.

FORFEIT

SPORT
ANSWERS & FORFEITS

Set 1

1 *Sandy Lyle*
2 *Brian Close*
3 *Ian Botham*
4 *Rugby League*
5 *Chris Woods*
6 *Derek Randall*
7 *Robinsons*
8 *Rugby Union*
9 *Evonne Goolagong*
10 *The FA Cup*

Impersonate a football manager explaining a home defeat. If you choose Ron Atkinson you must supply your own jewellery.

Set 2

1 *Glamorgan*
2 *Frank McAvennie*
3 *3*
4 *Modern pentathlon*
5 *Dickie*
6 *Mats Wilander*
7 *Le Mans*
8 *Foxhunting*
9 *Brothers*
10 *Dutch*

Sing a rugby song while standing on one leg.

Set 3

1 *He scored a duck (i.e. 0)*
2 *Australia*
3 *Barry McGuigan*
4 *Daley Thompson*
5 *Jonah Barrington*
6 *Ian Rush*
7 *Arsenal*

8 *Nijinsky*
9 *The Boat Race*
10 *Sheffield*

Imitate a famous bowler's run-up. Continue until at least one person has guessed who you're imitating.

Set 4

1 *Judo*
2 *Red*
3 *Ireland*
4 *John Hollins*
5 *Tennis (Boris Becker – Wimbledon)*
6 *East Germany*
7 *A quintuple tie*
8 *First-class cricket*
9 *The Tour de France*
10 *Norwich City*

Employing all the memory you can muster, realistically re-enact on the carpet the England Rugby Union team's last try.

Set 5

1 *Vitas Gerulaitis*
2 *Italy*
3 *A Russian degree*
4 *Keith Fletcher*
5 *Wales*
6 *John Conteh*
7 *Great Britain*
8 *England*
9 *Leicester*
10 *Sunil Gavaskar*

For one minute, mimic the famous sports commentator of your choice.

Set 6

1 *Bradford (Park Avenue)*
2 *The 1,000 Guineas, the Oaks and the St Leger*
3 *Barry Sheene*
4 *Richie Benaud*
5 *Virginia Holgate*
6 *Mike Brearley*
7 *Roger Taylor*
8 *Australia*
9 *Five*
10 *Yugoslavia*

Imitate the boxer of your choice explaining to Harry Carpenter why you have just lost a title fight.

Set 7

1 *Five*
2 *Ipswich Town*
3 *B*
4 *Mike Denness*
5 *He fell*
6 *1958 and 1970*
7 *Rugby League's*
8 *Graham Marsh (brother: Rod)*
9 *Nine*
10 *None*

Invite one of the other players to re-enact Ian Botham's walk from John O'Groats to Lands End. You must play the policeman who gets in his way.

Set 8

1 *Derek Pringle*
2 *Belgium*
3 *Phillipe Edmonds' wife (Frances)*
4 *1977*
5 *1985 (Kevin Moran)*
6 *Colin Dowdeswell*
7 *West Indies*

8 *Wales*
9 *Cliff Thorburn*
10 *Alan Glazier*

Select a partner and re-enact a typical dialogue between John McEnroe and an umpire. You must play the umpire.

Set 9

1 *None*
2 *Howard Clark*
3 *Mike Gatting (brother: Steve)*
4 *Ian Botham*
5 *Ray Reardon*
6 *Brian Clough*
7 *Tennis*
8 *Poland*
9 *Jose-Maria Canizares*
10 *Real (Royal) Tennis*

Standing on your head, name ten Football League clubs currently in the First Division.

Set 10

1 *Rugby and Eton*
2 *Wales*
3 *They won the English Cross-Country Championship*
4 *Fog*
5 *None*
6 *Joe Di Maggio*
7 *Third Lanark*
8 *Gordon Brand*
9 *Richard Hadlee*
10 *He wasn't Welsh*

Do one proper sit-up with a half-full glass of water on your chest.

FORFEIT

CONNECTIONS ANSWERS & FORFEITS

Set 1

1 *All won the Eurovision Song Contest*
2 *London Underground stations*
3 *All members of Enid Blyton's 'Famous Five'*
4 *Can all be followed by the word 'chase'*
5 *'De' can be added to all to make famous names*
6 *Famous men whose first name is Robert*
7 The Young Ones
8 *Can all be prefaced by the word 'Rugby'*
9 *Men knighted for services to soccer*
10 *(Surnames of actors in)* Hi De Hi

Say the word 'goolies' in five different ways.

Set 2

1 *T.E. Lawrence (of Arabia)*
2 *House-builders*
3 *Have all written books for children*
4 *Ford*
5 *Seasons*
6 *(The first names of) female newsreaders*
7 *Have all co-presented* That's Life
8 *(The first names of) the Monkees*
9 *Shakespeare characters*
10 *Have all been to prison*

'Gurn' (i.e. pull a daft face) for 30 seconds.

Set 3

1 *Sir Richard Attenborough*
2 *(First names of members or former members of) the Rolling Stones*
3 *Chocolate bars*
4 *(All can be followed by) 'British Empire'*
5 *Building societies*
6 *Grade family (including Delfont, Lew and Leslie's brother)*
7 *Editors of* The Times

8 *Prince*
9 The Saint *(Simon Templar)*
10 *(The second names of) famous shops or stores*

Make four identifiably different animal noises.

Set 4

1 *Brands of cigarettes*
2 *(Famous Sixties) disc jockeys*
3 *(The first names of) US Presidents' First Ladies*
4 *Have all written lyrics for popular songs*
5 *Have all been associated with* Private Eye
6 *(The first names of) former members of Mrs Thatcher's Cabinet*
7 *(The first names of) the Goons*
8 *Thatcher*
9 *Omar Khayyam*
10 *Popes*

Do an impersonation of a famous drunk (or a drunken famous person) arguing to a policeman that they are not over the limit.

Set 5

1 *Characters in* Dynasty
2 *Wives of Henry VIII*
3 *Characters in 'Cluedo'*
4 *Journalists*
5 *Regulars on* Hancock's Half-Hour
6 *(First names of) Elizabeth Taylor's husbands*
7 *Films directed by Peter Yates*
8 *(The first names of) the Oxford Group of poets*
9 *(First names of) people in line to the throne*
10 *Have all presented chat-shows*

Invite someone to blindfold you and turn you around a few times. Now find your way to the loo.

Set 6

1 *Mia Farrow*
2 *Parliamentary constituencies of Prime Ministers*
3 *(Can all be prefaced by the word) New*
4 *Have all had Number One hits*
5 *Towns on the River Thames*
6 *Politicians who have represented more than one party in Parliament*
7 *(Names or part of names of) butterflies*
8 *Bowls*
9 *Spring flowers*
10 *Can all be prefaced by the word 'house'*

Re-enact the Andrex commercial – and then clear up the toiletpaper.

Set 7

1 *(Anagrams of) screen monsters*
2 *Former BBC TV Controllers*
3 *(First names of) former heads of nationalised industries*
4 *(First names of) Liberal MPs*
5 *Countries occupied by the Nazis during World War II*
6 *Field Marshals*
7 *Characters (or former characters) in* Crossroads
8 *Jackson*
9 *Apostles*
10 *The London School of Economics (LSE)*

Sit through the next set of questions with an ice-cube in your undies.

Set 8

1 *(Parts of names of) properties on the 'Monopoly' board*
2 *Hughes*
3 *Cricketers who have been knighted*
4 *Letters worth four points in 'Scrabble'*
5 *Capital cities in Latin America*
6 *Varieties of mushrooms*
7 *(First names of) Formula One motor-racing champions*

8 *(The first names of) the original* Not the Nine O'Clock News *stars*
9 *Ryan O'Neal*
10 *Participants in the Westland saga*

If you're a man, put on make-up; if you're a woman, take off your make-up.

Set 9

1 *Murray*
2 *(First names of) broadcasting children of broadcasters*
3 *Anthony Newley*
4 *Devil*
5 *Welsh international sportsmen*
6 *Lady Antonia Fraser*
7 *(Famous people with the surname) Smith*
8 *The most valuable colours in snooker*
9 *(Original flavours of) Opal Fruits*
10 *(First names of) World Heavyweight boxing champions*

Submit to intense tickling for 30 seconds.

Set 10

1 *(First names of) famous people with colours in their surnames*
2 *All words that have featured in film titles*
3 *Football League clubs with 'X' in their title (NB: Crewe Alexandra)*
4 *(First names of) people associated with the National Theatre*
5 *(First names of) people involved in political scandals*
6 *All, at least once, finished second in the Grand National*
7 *(First names of) New Zealand cricket captains*
8 *Places which feature in the titles of bestselling books or novels*
9 *(First names of) British winners of the Hollywood Best Actor Oscar*
10 *(First names of) famous people with prominent teeth*

Drink a cup of tea or coffee with five sugars (or saccharin, if you prefer).

FORFEIT
MUSIC
ANSWERS & FORFEITS

Set 1

1 *Lionel Richie*
2 *76*
3 *Dave Stewart*
4 *James Taylor*
5 *Sade*
6 *Marty Wilde (daughter: Kim)*
7 *Peter (and the Wolf)*
8 *Micky Dolenz*
9 *Sacha Distel*
10 *'Underneath the Arches'*

Sing along to the record of your choice.

Set 2

1 *Billy Preston*
2 *George Gershwin*
3 *Bruce Springsteen's*
4 *'These Foolish Things'*
5 *'Great balls of fire!'*
6 *'Still'*
7 *Madonna*
8 *Peter and Gordon*
9 *Marvin Gaye*
10 *'Blockbuster'*

Using a tennis or squash racquet, 'play guitar' to the record of your choice.

Set 3

1 *'How Do You Sleep?'*
2 *Steve Winwood*
3 *Sting*
4 *Larry Adler*
5 *Rod Stewart*
6 *'Favour'*
7 *'The Last Post'*

8 *Wham!*
9 *Bobbysoxers*
10 *Black*

Sing a verse and chorus of any song from *The Sound of Music* – and look as though you're enjoying it.

Set 4

1 *'Shout'*
2 Camelot
3 *A zither*
4 *The Animals*
5 *The Sultans of Swing*
6 *Neil Diamond*
7 *Bill Wyman*
8 *Sheena Easton*
9 *'All the Way'*
10 *Larry Parnes*

Do an impersonation of Mick Jagger singing 'Strangers in the Night'.

Set 5

1 *San Francisco*
2 *'In a railway station'*
3 *The Silver Bullet Band*
4 *Them*
5 *'Chocolate cake'*
6 *1944*
7 *Alexei Sayle ('Ullo John, gotta new motor?')*
8 *Arcadia*
9 *'Buddy [or brother], can you spare a dime?'*
10 *Grateful Dead*

Do an impersonation of Bruce Springsteen singing 'When I'm 64'.

MUSIC
ANSWERS & FORFEITS

Set 6

1 *John Entwhistle*
2 *'Where my Rosemary goes'*
3 *Steve Strange*
4 *U2 (Bono)*
5 *Mars (The Bringer of War)*
6 *Lulu*
7 *'Haitian Divorce'*
8 *'Your Song'*
9 *Crosby, Stills and Nash*
10 *(Corky) Laing*

Imitate the sound of bagpipes for 30 seconds (or less if the assembled company can't take it anymore).

Set 7

1 *Rory Bremner*
2 *Jimmy Young*
3 *Velvet Underground*
4 *Bruce Springsteen*
5 *Joni Mitchell*
6 *'Clowns'*
7 *Steve Ellis*
8 *Crystal Gayle*
9 *Kiri Te Kanawa*
10 *Johnny B. Goode*

Sing the National Anthem backwards (the words not the letters).

Set 8

1 *Charles Manson*
2 *Leonard Cohen* (Songs of Love and Hate)
3 Pictures at an Exhibition
4 *'The Power of Love'*
5 Carousel
6 *'I don't exist'*
7 *Richard Wagner*

8 *'Babooshka'*
9 *Pennsylvania 6-5000*
10 *'Little Green Apples'*

Ask someone to play some music for 30 seconds; if you are over 30, you must breakdance to it, if you are under 30, you must tap-dance.

Set 9

1 *Terry*
2 *Paul Whiteman's*
3 *Xylophone*
4 *Mama Cass*
5 *20,066 (4,000 – 'A Day in the Life'; '5 4 3 2 1'; 'Route 66')*
6 *Amadeus*
7 *Robert Burns*
8 *Yazoo*
9 *Finchley Central*
10 *Hotel California*

Sing the song of your choice while gargling with water.

Set 10

1 *Wimpole Street*
2 *Their first three records all went to Number One*
3 *Jimmy Saville*
4 *Artie Shaw*
5 *Gil Scott-Heron*
6 *20 ('24 Hours From Tulsa'; 'Two Little Boys'; 'Eight Days a Week')*
7 *Toyah (she married Robert Fripp, co-founder of King Crimson)*
8 *Elvis Costello*
9 *Labi Siffre*
10 *Stevie Nicks*

Whistle any advertising jingle while someone peels an orange. If you fail, eat the orange and repeat the process until you succeed (or until you run out of oranges).

FORFEIT

POLITICS
ANSWERS & FORFEITS

Set 1

1 *Bill Rodgers*
2 *Plaid Cymru*
3 *Michael Foot*
4 *Hilda*
5 *The Labour majority in 1945*
6 *Derek Hatton*
7 *Edward Kennedy*
8 *Secretary of State for Scotland*
9 *The Conservative Party*
10 *The Conservative Party*

Tell a joke about the politician of your choice.

Set 2

1 *James Callaghan*
2 *Francis Pym*
3 *Six*
4 *Bernie Grant*
5 *The Transport & General Workers Union*
6 *Roy Jenkins*
7 *The Liberal Party*
8 *Huddersfield Town*
9 *Lobby Correspondents*
10 *The Labour Party*

Draw a cartoon of a famous politician. If no one can guess the subject of your cartoon, draw another one (and so on).

Set 3

1 *David Lange*
2 *James Callaghan*
3 *397*
4 *Norman Tebbit*
5 *The Conservative Party*
6 *Roy Hattersley*
7 *Barbara Castle*

8 *The Democratic Unionist Party*
9 A Week in Politics
10 *Vic Feather*

Imitate a politician explaining why their party has lost a key by-election.

Set 4

1 *Matthew Parris*
2 *The Monday Club*
3 *Johnson Matthey*
4 *Robert McKenzie*
5 *1970*
6 *Jeffrey Archer*
7 *John Pardoe*
8 *Oppenheim*
9 *Robert Kilroy-Silk*
10 *Paddy Ashdown*

In one minute, summarise either the next Conservative or Labour election manifesto, or, if you prefer, take ten seconds to summarise the Alliance manifesto.

Set 5

1 *Secretary of State for Northern Ireland*
2 *The National Front*
3 *Michael Heseltine*
4 *Ramsay McDonald*
5 *Actor*
6 *The Democrat Party*
7 *Ian Mikardo*
8 *David Steel*
9 *Benjamin Disraeli (Dizzy)*
10 *François Mitterrand*

For one minute, imitate the political commentator of your choice.

Set 6

1 *Four*
2 *The Labour Party*
3 *Harold Macmillan*
4 *The Third Reading*
5 *Gerry Adams*
6 *The Labour Party*
7 *Felipe Gonzales*
8 *Eugene McCarthy*
9 *John Cleese*
10 *Harriet Harman*

Offer the Labour Party policy on the EEC while doing press-ups (minimum 30 seconds please).

Set 7

1 *Sir Geoffrey Howe*
2 *Jo Grimond*
3 *Defence Secretary*
4 *Selwyn Lloyd*
5 *Leo Abse*
6 *Anthony Eden*
7 *Lincoln*
8 *Five*
9 *Llin Golding (his wife)*
10 *Tim Sainsbury*

Ask someone to select a novel and then you must read the first page in the voice of the Prime Minister.

Set 8

1 *1965*
2 *Bedwellty*
3 *Tony Banks*
4 *Canada*
5 *Adjournment Debate*
6 *Jack Ashley*
7 *Richard Tracey*

8 *Six*
9 *New York*
10 *Anthony Crosland*

Do an impression of the Rev. Ian Paisley complaining to the Electricity Board about the size of his electricity bill.

Set 9

1 *Richard Crossman*
2 *Randolph (2)*
3 *The Scottish Nationalist Party*
4 *Colin Moynihan*
5 *Graham Tope*
6 *None*
7 *David Lloyd George*
8 *James Callaghan*
9 *Gwyneth Dunwoody*
10 *Laurent Fabius*

Standing on one leg summarise the Election Manifesto of the Official Monster Raving Loony Party.

Set 10

1 *300*
2 *Dean Rusk*
3 *He made the longest filibuster*
4 *Helmut Schmidt*
5 *Leon Brittan*
6 *Jomo Kenyatta (Peter)*
7 *William McKinley (1901)*
8 *£400*
9 *Sir Keith Joseph, Willie Hamilton, Edward Heath, Enoch Powell*
10 *October 1974*

Imitate the politician of your choice addressing a meeting. Invite the assembled company to heckle you and throw rotten fruit, cold water etc.